Ernest Myers

Lord Althorp

Ernest Myers

Lord Althorp

ISBN/EAN: 9783743337329

Manufactured in Europe, USA, Canada, Australia, Japa

Cover: Foto ©ninafisch / pixelio.de

Manufactured and distributed by brebook publishing software (www.brebook.com)

Ernest Myers

Lord Althorp

BY

ERNEST MYERS.

LONDON:
RICHARD BENTLEY AND SON,
Publishers in Ordinary to Her Majesty the Queen.
1890.

(All rights reserved.)

PREFACE.

NEARLY fourteen years ago there was published a most interesting memoir of Lord Althorp, written by the late Sir Denis Le Marchant, formerly Clerk of the House of Commons, who had died more than a year before the publication of his book. Besides many other qualifications for the work, the author had the peculiar and inestimable advantage of having been the private secretary and intimate friend of the man whose life he described. His book must, therefore, always have an unique value, and must remain the necessary foundation of all others on the same subject. But it was, as its preface states, "originally intended only for private circulation among the members of Lord Althorp's family," and thus differs in some respects from books meant only for the general public. And though it was published in 1876, it was mostly written a good deal before that date, when there were many public men still living who had known Althorp personally and joined in his political action. These, again, would, some twenty or thirty years ago, form an audience of whom his biographer would have special regard; now they are dwindled to a very small handful. It has, therefore, seemed to me that a fresh attempt to help in keeping alive among his countrymen the memory of a man so emphatically an "English worthy," may be accounted no longer superfluous; and that this attempt may be best made in a short and what is called popular form.

I cannot but think that consideration of the critical epoch in which Althorp was a political leader, leads to a higher estimate than that perhaps commonly current of the importance of the part played by him in the events which then helped to shape the destiny of our commonwealth. This is, of course, matter of opinion, and it is the concern of this book briefly to recount the facts on which opinion may be formed. But even if readers of the book do not wholly accept its conclusions, they may at least not regret time spent on the contemplation of a career and character pure and honest and self-denying to a degree seldom found in the political life of any State.

Histories, memoirs, essays, and other books narrating or illustrating the events of Althorp's time are numerous, easily accessible, and mostly well known; so that an enumeration of all the records consulted, or reference to them in footnotes, would appear out of due proportion to the size of this volume. Lord Spencer has kindly lent me a large collection of his uncle's letters to and from William the Fourth, Lord Grey, Lord Brougham, and the second Earl Spencer, Althorp's father. The most interesting of these letters were selected and given at length by Sir Denis Le Marchant in his memoir.

E. M.

February, 1890.

CONTENTS.

CHAPTER		PAGE
I.	Early Life	1
II.	First Action in Parliament	18
III.	Marriage and Bereavement—Leadership of the Liberal Opposition	34
IV.	Acceptance of Office and Leadership of the House of Commons	56
V.	The First Reform Bill	72
VI.	The Reform Act	84
VII.	First Year of the Reformed Parliament	116
VIII.	Second Year of the Reformed Parliament	157
IX.	Retirement and Last Years	202
X.	Retrospect and Prospect	215

ERRATA.

Page 63, line 7, *for* "notion" *read* "motion."
,, 75 ,, 14, *for* "measures" *read* "measure."
,, 107 ,, 2, *for* "intervals" *read* "interval."

LORD ALTHORP.

Τὸ δέ που ἀληθὲς ὧδ᾽ ἔχει· ἐν πόλει ᾗ ἥκιστα πρόθυμοι ἄρχειν οἱ μέλλοντες ἄρξειν, ταύτην ἄριστα καὶ ἀστασιαστότατα ἀνάγκη οἰκεῖσθαι, τὴν δ᾽ ἐναντίους ἄρχοντας σχοῦσαν ἐναντίως.

"For the truth of the matter is this: that State in which the rulers are least eager to rule must needs be the best and most harmoniously ordered; and the more eager the rulers, the worse for the State."—PLATO's *Republic*, book vii. p. 520 D.

CHAPTER I.

EARLY LIFE.

WHATEVER may be the defects of Parliamentary government, there can be no question that it forms the mainspring of the political system of this country; and the history of the British Parliament is in constant relation to the larger history of the British Empire. The epochs, therefore, at which our Parliamentary system has been profoundly modified, have a great and peculiar interest; and of such epochs none has on the whole been more momentous than that which is recorded in the statute-book by the Reform Act of 1832. The labours of many men joined in that achievement, and perhaps not any one of them can be called absolutely indispensable to its success. But if there be any men of whom that might with great measure of reason be said, one of those men is without doubt Lord Althorp, leader of the House of Commons from November, 1830, to November, 1834. Even if it be allowed that the Reform Act would have passed without him, it was at least very largely due to him that it passed in peace and order, and left no embittering memories behind.

No truthful biography can be a mere panegyric, but there are few men of whom there is so little save good to tell; few men, and still fewer politicians. The truth is that while in political work there has often been exercise of very high intellectual faculties, there is seldom anything morally heroic discoverable in a political career. We are apt, perhaps, to be sometimes dazzled by the pomp of its attendant circumstance.

> "The applause of listening senates to command,
> The threats of pain and ruin to despise,
> To scatter plenty o'er a smiling land,
> And read their history in a nation's eyes,"

—all this attracts an excited admiration which is disposed, by a not unnatural illusion, to idealize the figures of historic statesmen. The higher forms of heroism belong, in reality, to struggles where more of unrecompensed devotion is possible; to the perils of war and of the sea, of pestilence or of fire, with countless other trials and labours of private life, in which unremembered men and women have shown far nobler qualities than such as any political occasion whatsoever can call forth. A statesman, if he succeeds for his country, succeeds also for himself, and reaps the first and amplest rewards of his own services. If he fails, the "pain and ruin" fall more heavily on others than on him. If he removes an injustice, it can hardly be until the labours of other men, his precursors, have secured him a repayment in the shape of popular support. The efforts of virtue that may be required of him are of a kind which in other fields might be thought rather negative than positive; honesty, firmness, vigilance on behalf of interests with which his own are inseparably bound up. But if these virtues are somewhat elementary, they are by no means for that reason too common among politicians, as the present generation of Englishmen have good reason to know; and their absence or presence in the leaders of a nation may make momentous difference to that nation's life.

It is as an illustration of the priceless value of character in a statesman that Althorp's memory is first and foremost to be cherished; and with this are connected other points of signal interest to the student of British and of Parliamentary history. It is surely worthy of remark, and, I would say, of admiration, that in the House of Commons, a popular assembly of debate, and in a time of profound changes and agitations, the leadership was by common consent assigned to a man altogether devoid of rhetorical arts, legitimate and illegitimate alike. The authority assigned to the Duke of Wellington was also in part a tribute to that single-mindedness in which he equalled Althorp; but Wellington did not sit in the House of Commons, and his integrity was linked to the greatest and most glorious name among men then living on the earth.

With this single-mindedness were joined in Althorp the political sagacity, almost as much instinctive as reasoned, and the unswerving resolution which made him a power in the State. He took long to make up his mind, as behoves a statesman, even when quicker-witted than he; but once pledged to a policy, he never failed to stand to his guns. And with this constancy he com-

bined a quality wanting in some resolute men—
or, at least, in men whose eagerness looks like
resolution—the quality, namely, of an ample and
wise patience, rejecting the short cuts to triumph
which dazzle self-confident and thwarted poli-
ticians with their deadly lure. But the thing
that makes him virtually unique among statesmen
is this—that what so many public men say of
themselves (and in intervals of weariness doubt-
less say truly) was absolutely and always true
of him—that he immensely preferred a private
to a public life, and only endured office as a
labour which the voice of duty enjoined. There
need be nothing, of course, dishonourable in
political ambition and the love of power, if
they be mingled with high public aims. But the
temptations of ambition, even in good men, are
obvious; obvious, that is, in a general sense,
though it is by no means obvious how many
subtle forms they may take. It is no less plain
how, in troublous times, men's confidence must
be gained, and their political efforts calmed and
ennobled, when they can be assured of finding in
their rulers the transparent disinterestedness and
self-sacrifice with which Althorp wielded power
against his will. In him was fulfilled that ancient

postulate of Plato's ideal commonwealth which stands as the motto of this book.

John Charles Spencer, known for the greater part of his life by the courtesy title of Viscount Althorp, was born in London, at Spencer House, on the 30th of May, 1782. His father, the second Earl Spencer, was First Lord of the Admiralty in Pitt's ministry from 1793 to 1801, when he resigned with his chief on the refusal of the king to consent to Catholic Emancipation. He had, therefore, the honour of holding this office of supreme importance during eight of the most glorious years in the whole history of the British navy, and may claim at least a reflected lustre on his name from the victories of Howe and Hood, of Duncan and Jervis, of Collingwood and of Nelson. His administration of the navy contrasted to his credit with the contemporary administration of the army. He brought forward and supported the great admirals named above; and he showed a seemly care for the brave seamen who fought and conquered under them. In the alarming mutinies at the Nore and elsewhere on the coasts he acted with promptitude and firmness, and without panic; nor was he content to suppress the symptoms without touching the cause of the disorder. With the zealous co-operation of the best chiefs of the service, he visited the fleet, received the complaints of the sailors, improved their comfort, and by reformed regulation of their discipline did his best to secure them from arbitrary tyrannies. It is claimed for him that his radically reformed system is the basis on which the present administrative code of the navy has been built up.

Lord Spencer did not return to office in Pitt's last ministry, but after the death of Pitt he was Home Secretary in Lord Grenville's thirteen months' administration of 1806–7; and then quitted office, and the ambition of office, to live in comparative retirement the remaining twenty-seven years of his life. He was a scholar and student, the chief maker of one of the finest private libraries in the world, a kind and liberal landlord, a zealous agriculturist; but his extravagance in the management of his property became, as will be afterwards seen, the chief cause of his son's ultimate withdrawal from public life.

Althorp had reason to be proud of his mother as well as of his father. She was the Lavinia Bingham (eldest daughter of Lord Lucan, a friend of Johnson and Burke) who was painted by Reynolds in several well-known and beautiful portraits; and her heart and mind seem to have been not unworthy of her face. In 1795, some fourteen years after their marriage, the Spencers visited Gibbon at Lausanne, and he describes Lady Spencer in a letter as "a charming woman, who, with sense and spirit, has the playfulness and simplicity of a child." During her husband's tenure of office she aided him by her intelligence and her charm, and made his house attractive to the distinguished men with whom his office brought him into contact. Yet, notwithstanding the good qualities of both these parents, there seems to be no doubt that from their absorption in business and society they grievously neglected the personal supervision of their eldest son's development of his faculties. Althorp, in a brief fragment of autobiography, to which reference will again be made, speaks strongly of the deficiencies of his education. He was taught to read by a Swiss footman, who appears to have been his only instructor till he was sent off to Harrow at the cruelly early age of eight. It was, however, more habitual then to send boys very young to public schools; and perhaps the evil of this premature banishment from home was somewhat neutralized by that very neglect of his childhood which had accustomed him to take care of himself. His love of field-sports must have helped also to this end. Among his father's papers was found a letter in which little Jack describes a morning's sport enjoyed by him at the age of seven.* This passion for rural pursuits, with all its advantages and delights, had the disadvantage also of throwing him in his childhood somewhat too much with the illiterate. Before he left home, his portrait was painted by Reynolds —a charming picture of a right English little boy.

At Harrow he was not specially distinguished, but held his own in work and play, was steady, happy, more industrious than the average schoolboy, and made some good and lifelong friends. His fag-

---

* The letter runs thus :—

"DEAR PAPA,

"I went to Brington Hill this morning, and catched four rabbits, and there was a good many people; and I did not know who they were all.

"We threw off at ten o'clock. Tartar and Bowler, and Punch and Turpin, did very well; but Jenny's puppy did not do well, for she cried at the bushes. Fanny did very well too. I rode on Castlebar, and Ned Corns was behind; John Townshend and James walked by me, and I went a gallop and had good sport. When you come back there is to be a race, in which you are to run; and so shall John Townshend, and Jack Corns, and Peter. I am to ride on Ginger, and you shall ride on Cowslip. I got these horses at the races at Northampton, and yours is a very good one. You have been a long time away. So no more.

"JACK SPENCER, VISCOUNT ALTHORP."

master there, named Hodges, afterwards member for Kent, described him in his first year as "a quiet bashful boy, with great sweetness of temper, and eminently truthful." Like many English boys, he wanted to go into the navy; but Lord Spencer thought this a younger son's profession, and kept it for Althorp's brothers, Robert and Frederick. In his seventeenth year, having duly reached the highest form in the school, Althorp left Harrow, and after a wasted half-year's attempt at special preparation for the university with an inefficient clergyman as tutor, he went up to Trinity College, Cambridge, in January, 1800.

At Cambridge he only spent a little more than two years, and with much less profit than he might have derived if his own wish to improve himself had not been thwarted by the absurd and wantonly mischievous regulations of the university which seem to have been then in force. If an undergraduate happened to be the son or brother of a peer, he was at that time not only allowed to take an ordinary degree without examination, and after only two years' residence, but he was actually debarred from entering for the "honour" examinations, which for the average English student, not born a specialist in letters or science, might, with all their faults, be called not unfairly the chief guide and impulse in the intellectual part of a university education.* The only kind of "honours" open to Althorp, a first class in the yearly examination of his college, he gained by hard work, in great part to gratify his mother, who told him that she had set her heart on his achieving this solitary academic distinction accessible to him. He was not only in this first class among men of the second year, but also stood first in the class, being placed above men who were afterwards high Wranglers and Fellows of the college. It is not very often that the heir to a peerage is qualified for an open Fellowship at Oxford or Cambridge. But Althorp's high place in this examination was won chiefly by mathematics, and he had comparatively little of the classical scholarship which so deeply saturated the minds of Fox, Pitt, Canning, Peel, and so many other English statesmen of that age. It seems, indeed, much to be regretted that one who was himself in many ways so like one of "Plutarch's men" should not have enjoyed a closer intercourse

---

* This exclusion has, of course, long ago ended, and it might now be said with some truth that the two classes of men to whom university honours are of most service in after-life are schoolmasters and political peers.

with the spirit of the Greek and Roman commonwealths with which he had so much in common. In his preference of mathematics and, subsequently, of political economy as his most seriously pursued studies, he may remind the present generation of Henry Fawcett, in whose mind and character other resemblances might be found to his. We do, indeed, find him writing to his father two years hence from Rome, after visiting churches and galleries, "But I have read a thing which has given me much greater pleasure than any of these things; it is Demosthenes' oration 'De Chersoneso,' which is far the finest specimen of eloquence I have ever seen." To read Demosthenes with enjoyment argues no inconsiderable amount of Greek scholarship. But, among all the masterpieces of Greek and Latin poetry, the only work for which he seems to have shown real love was the "Georgics" of Virgil; and this was the fondness of a lover of rural things at least as much as of a lover of poetry.

Short and maimed as this spell of university life was, it was of undoubted use to Althorp. Besides the intellectual training and companionship, to so modest a man as he it was a needful encouragement to find, by success in an academic examination, that he possessed abilities of any kind above the average. For the moment, indeed, his progress was checked, and worse than checked. Under the sedulous discouragement of his studies by the university, he not unnaturally turned to amusement; and for a few months devoted himself not merely to the hunting-field, where he was known as one of the hardest riders, but also to the turf. Happily this was but a brief madness, and after one season's disastrous experience he forswore racing for ever. His grandfather, the first earl, had been an incurable gambler, and it might have been feared that the vice was in the grandson's blood, and would taint his life. No life, from this year onward, could have been more free from it than his.

His time at Cambridge was too short, especially for so retiring a man as Althorp, to allow adequate opportunity for forming the friendships which are, as is commonly and truly said, the best fruit of university life. But those friends that he did make were good, and among them, in spite of his mother's injunction to "beware of Whigs," were Lord Ebrington and Lord Henry Petty, afterwards Lord Lansdowne, both eminent among his future political allies.

On taking his degree and leaving Cambridge, he

travelled on the Continent with another young man, related to Lady Spencer's family, from the autumn of 1802 to the spring of 1803, when the short Peace of Amiens ended abruptly, and they had to come home. His parents had hoped that travel, with good introductions, would do something to give him the readiness and polish which he declined to acquire in London society. But his foreign tour was altogether premature. He could speak neither French nor Italian, and knew little or nothing of those languages. Of the art, and the greater part of the history, of the lands in which he travelled, he was scarcely less ignorant. In after-life, when he regretted his lost opportunities, he could only recall one benefit from his visit to France and Italy. The sight of the oppression of free thought in Italy brought home to his mind the wrong of sectarian "ascendencies;" and his first spontaneously conceived political conviction was that which formed the chief honour of the Whig party—the conviction of the evils of religious intolerance. But in social accomplishments he returned no better fitted than he had set out, and no better disposed, for the brilliant assemblies of Spencer House. "He detested," he said, "the life of a grandee." His father, however, did not despair of him, and after a year's interval procured him an introduction into the political life which was ultimately to discipline him into the leading and controlling spirit of a peaceful revolution. Althorp was, in fact, one of those men (and they are not to be lightly prized) on whom public responsibilities must be thrust almost against their will, and who will then fulfil them to the uttermost. It was rather to please his parents than from any ambition of his own that he took the first steps of his political career. Pitt found his old friend's son a seat for the nomination borough of Okehampton; and in April, 1804, toward the close of his twenty-second year, Althorp entered the House of Commons.

In January, 1806, Pitt died; next month Lord Grenville's ministry of "all the talents" came into office, and parties and public men fell suddenly into new relations and adjustments at this shock to the political kaleidoscope. Lord Spencer took office as Home Secretary, thus definitely ranging himself again with the Whig party, now beginning to reunite itself after the disruption which followed the outbreak of the Revolution in France. Not only did he procure his son a junior lordship of the Treasury, but oddly enough he insisted on his giving up Okehampton and standing for the University of Cambridge, in opposition to his friend Lord Henry Petty, to whom the Chancellorship of the Exchequer had been assigned. The only explanation of this eccentricity seems to be that it was not known at first that Petty would stand, and that the Spencers thought themselves bound to those electors who had already promised Althorp their support. At any rate, not the slightest ill feeling was caused; indeed, Althorp's candidature against a cabinet minister cannot have been taken very seriously by any one, least of all by himself. Petty was perfectly safe, and obtained more than double the number of votes given either to Althorp or to Palmerston, who was also contesting the seat, but in the Tory interest.

For the remainder of that Parliament another nomination borough (St. Alban's) was found for Althorp. But at the general election of November, 1806, he was brought forward for his own county of Northampton, and was elected by a small majority over the Tory candidate. He continued to sit for Northamptonshire twenty-eight years, the whole remaining term of his membership of the House of Commons.

The representation of a county may have seemed

to some a premature honour for so young a man, but it was the only ostensible honour in public life which Althorp was to hold for the next twenty-three years. In a few months Fox had followed his great rival into the silence of death; the Tories returned to power; the shadow of Napoleon loomed larger than ever over Europe; and England was once more absorbed in her struggle against foreign perils, for her own liberties and for those of the civilized world. She had no leisure for the home reforms demanded by the Whigs, and accepted, with all its defects, the party which promised stability amid the chaotic crash of continental violence and rapine.

CHAPTER II.

FIRST ACTION IN PARLIAMENT.

PITT was gone, but though Pitt to the last had called himself a Whig, the larger portion of his spirit was believed to have descended to the Tories, as being more in earnest in the vital struggle abroad. Neither party was rich in capable statesmen, but the most capable man, Canning, was on the Tory side. Owing to Cabinet quarrels, and not wholly without his own fault, Canning was only intermittently in office; but his two years and a half at the Foreign Office (March 25, 1807, to September 9, 1809) were of signal service to his country, mainly by the appointment of Sir Arthur Wellesley to the chief command of our army in the Peninsula. There was much to attract Althorp in the more actively patriotic party; and in the unformed state of his own convictions and party ties, and indeed of party ties in general in those years, he might very possibly have thrown in his lot with Pitt's disciple, as his father had done with Pitt. But in the year 1809 the House and the country were stirred by an affair which called forth Althorp's first pronounced political action, and had the effect of deciding his position among party organizations thenceforth.

The Duke of York, second son of George III., and commander-in-chief of the army, had been charged with having overlooked and even connived at the sale of military patronage by his mistress, Mrs. Clarke; and a Committee of the House of Commons was appointed to inquire into the charge. Colonel Wardle, his accuser, had to conduct the examination-in-chief of the witnesses, and was hopelessly mismanaging the case, when Whitbread, a "Democratic Whig," took it up, and examined to such purpose that the evidence thus placed on record made it virtually certain that sooner or later the Duke of York must give up his post. But this was not by any means apparent to the House immediately. Colonel Wardle's motion to address the Crown for the duke's removal was lost by a majority of 243. A small minority, however, had been already convinced that the duke must go, and were resolved to act on their convictions. One of these was Althorp.

It was not an attractive occasion for a young man to undertake his first active intervention in debate, unless indeed for one totally unlike Althorp. He was the most good-natured as well as the most unassuming of men, and the least likely to try to found a reputation on a personal attack. Besides this, the leaders of his party were still disposed to let the matter drop. All the Whig ex-ministers took this view. The duke was a genial and popular man, with many good qualities; and though he had no military ability, or claim to credit for improvements in army organization, he had not undeservedly obtained a reputation for solicitude for the welfare of the private soldier. He was also a friend of Lord Spencer, and had kept clear of political party ties, as befitted his rank and office. It is highly characteristic of Althorp's courage and honesty that it was in so distasteful a case that he first came prominently forward, simply because a man was needed to do what he thought ought to be done. Although the motion to address the Crown for the duke's removal had been lost, the arguments of the minority began to work on the consciences of vacillating members, and were strongly reinforced by a gathering tide of public opinion in the country. It was felt to be intolerable that a ministry which appealed for support on the ground of military efficiency should be allowed to countenance exposed military abuses. When Spencer Perceval, then Chancellor of the Exchequer, moved a resolution altogether exonerating the duke, even the House felt this to be going too far; not only the Whigs in a body, but some Tories also, joined in remonstrating; and the exculpating resolution was only passed in an amended form, which was virtually its defeat. The duke resigned. But to satisfy justice it was necessary that the causal connexion between his resignation and the inquiry into his conduct should be placed on record. Whitbread, feeling probably that he had himself been too much of an advocate before the committee to take the next step, looked round for a suitable lieutenant, and finally made choice of Althorp, who consented to undertake the task. For two sessions he had sat silent in the House, but his independence and absolute sincerity had already made themselves felt in private intercourse, and he was known to have strong convictions on this matter. The rank, birth, and influence of the culprit, which inclined many to pass over his offence, rightly seemed to Althorp additional reasons for marking it more emphatically. And if a blow was to be struck at corrupt privilege, then the more conspicuous the example the more enduring would be the effect. As the length of Althorp's maiden speech is not great, it may be quoted here for its characteristic directness and simplicity—a simplicity which never quite lost the mark of youthful ingenuousness most naturally appropriate to this time of his life. The speech is thus given in Hansard:—

"Lord Althorp said: 'That there were one or two positions advanced by the right honourable gentleman who had just sat down (Bathurst) in which he could not entirely concur. With regard to the regret of the right honourable gentleman for the resignation of the Duke of York, he admitted that it was a great loss to lose the services of those who had, while in office, efficiently discharged their duty; but the loss of the services of the Duke of York was considerably lessened, when they recollected in what manner it had been proved at their bar that the Royal Duke discharged his duty. He differed also from that right honourable gentleman as to the great use and importance he thought proper to attach to the elevated rank of that illustrious person. He (Lord Althorp) was rather disposed to think that such high rank and affinity to the throne were not the most recommendatory qualifications for the most responsible situations under the Crown; and he appealed to those who heard him, if, in the course of the late proceedings, their debates were not, in some degree, influenced by considerations of delicacy, inseparable from any discussion involving the character and honour of one so near his Majesty; and, therefore, it did appear to him to be of the greatest importance that no such person should, for the future, be called to such high situations but such as could be completely responsible. Another assertion of the right honourable gentleman went to the total acquittal of the Duke of York, as to corruption or connivance. It was not necessary now, perhaps, to go into this, but as it was mentioned, he would state that he did think the Duke of York had been proved guilty of connivance at the corrupt practices which had taken place; and, if his Royal Highness had continued in office, he thought that the House must have gone further, and passed a sentence upon him that would have rendered his resignation unavoidable. With regard to their subsequent proceedings, he was of opinion that the question stood in a state in which the House of Commons ought not to suffer it to remain. He wished to place it on the journals that the Duke of York had resigned. This notification would give consistency to the entire character of the proceeding, and bring it to its proper close, at the same time satisfactorily explaining why it was closed. Not, however, that he would be understood to say that he considered removal from office a constitutional punishment, but it would be, in this case, so far effective as to preclude the possibility of that Royal Duke being ever reappointed to a situation he had proved himself so incompetent to fill. No man could, or ought to hold that important situation, who was not in full possession of the confidence of the country. The Duke of York had forfeited that confidence. He had lost the confidence of the country for ever, and, by consequence, he must abandon all hopes of ever again returning to that situation. This was a severe lesson, but it was as salutary as it was severe; it would prove to all who might succeed that Royal Duke, that it was not within the power of any sovereign, however beloved or confided in, to protect his most favoured servant from the consequences of the maladministration of his public duty.' The noble lord then concluded by moving, 'That his Royal Highness the Duke of York having resigned the command of the army, this House does not now think it necessary to proceed any further in the consideration of the evidence before the Committee appointed to inquire into the conduct of his Royal Highness, as far as that evidence related to his Royal Highness the Duke of York.'"

With the omission of the word "now" (which was thought to imply the duke's permanent exclusion from public service) the resolution was allowed to pass without amendment, and a noteworthy victory was won for the cause of honest service of the State.

It was at this point, in the twenty-eighth year of his life and the fifth of his Parliamentary duties, that Althorp's political convictions took definite and effective shape. He writes to his father (March 18, 1809), "My political situation is very much changed within the last fortnight; my opinions, as you know, have long been the same, but till now I have never had the nerve to act on them."

It might be said with truth that at this time there were two great tasks for England, and that no one party by itself was adequate to both. Those tasks were foreign war and home reform.

If it be allowed that to pursue both with equal energy was too much for any one set of men, then there would seem to be some justification in this for our party-system, even at that critical time, when national unity was of transcendent importance, and anything that might even appear to impair it was proportionately dangerous. Some members of the Whig party cannot be acquitted on the charge of having sometimes embarrassed the Government during the great combat against Napoleon, though from this charge we may altogether exempt Althorp. He had, however, now thrown in his lot with those who were resolved that home needs should not be neglected. To them also belonged a part, and no unimportant part, in the work of national defence. It was of little use to repel the encroaching flames of revolution and tyranny abroad, if materials for internal conflagration were suffered to be heaped up by unreformed abuses at home.

Since the death of Fox in 1806, this party had neither an effective head nor effective unity among themselves. Their "natural leaders," the elder members of great Whig houses, were at this time mostly held by Althorp and his friends to be lacking in earnestness and clearness of sight. Grey himself, the future Prime Minister of Reform, had hung back in the matter of the Duke of York. The man who had then shown the way to the Whigs, Samuel Whitbread, the great brewer, was now recognized as leader of the more resolute reformers. His wife was Grey's sister, but he had studiously maintained independence of the Whig nobles, undoubtedly from good motives and with good result, but it would seem also with something of ostentatious insistence. His fault seems to have been a tendency to an over-obtrusion of his own personality, which somewhat marred the effect of his undoubted disinterestedness and public spirit. Except to attentive students of the political history of those times, his name is very possibly known chiefly now through the references to him in "Rejected Addresses," and by the burlesque oration in verse which was put into his mouth by Canning—

"I'm like Archimedes for science and skill,
I'm like a young prince going straight up a hill," etc.

This was a paraphrastic parody of Whitbread's speech when, in 1805, he proposed the impeachment of Lord Melville for misappropriation of public funds in his office of Treasurer of the Navy. Soon after Melville's disgrace Pitt died, and the Grenville ministry was formed. Many supposed that Whitbread would be in the new Cabinet. Indeed, Fox took it as a matter of course, and said familiarly, *more suo*, to Grey, "What office is Sam to have?" Grey unfortunately took upon himself to answer, without consulting his brother-in-law, that he knew he would not accept office, and Fox and Grenville acquiesced without making the proposal to the person concerned. "Sam" was naturally displeased both that Grey's reply on his behalf should have been made, and also that it should have been accepted as final in the matter; nor was his displeasure diminished by the offer of a peerage, which he declined with disgust. He was of too generous a nature to feel vindictiveness, but, as was to be expected, this incident disposed him more than ever to take his own line; and his following began to assume the character of what, in the phrase of continental assemblies, is called the Extreme Left. In the censure of the Duke of York he found an opportunity of signalizing his warfare on public abuses. But he by no means confined his attention to such as would confer celebrity on their assailant, but laboured at the no less needful but less conspicuous work of reform in prisons and lunatic asylums. In his command of the Bedfordshire militia he was energetic and strict almost to a fault. He was no demagogue, and seems never to have stooped to flattery or bribery of "the masses," on whose behalf he toiled. He was unselfish, though by no means self-forgetting.*

Next to Whitbread in this group stood Sir Samuel Romilly, less active in debate, but building himself a more enduring fame by his reforms of the law. After these came younger lieutenants—Sir Francis Burdett, Lord Folkestone, Lord Archibald Hamilton, Lord Milton—all displaying some eccentricity in their impatience of political conventionalities, all animated by ardent zeal for an improvement of the condition of the poor. To these men Althorp joined himself, and was content to accept with them the name of Radical which their disapprovers gave them—a name now appearing for the first time in our political history.

There does not seem to be any speech or writing extant in which Althorp has explained the precise significance in which he accepted this name, but the whole tenor of his political life makes this as plain as any verbal definition or explanation could

* See a biographic note on Whitbread in pp. 172–180 of Sir D. Le Marchant's book.

make it. There are two senses in which a man may be called a Radical, or "root-man." It may mean that he is persuaded to see advantage in whatever detaches or severs the roots of an ancient polity and society from the soil of custom and tradition which has nourished it. In this case, if he differs from a Revolutionary, it is only in the point—an important one, doubtless—that he does not necessarily think that this detachment must be accomplished violently or even suddenly. But a Radical of a different kind may justify his name by holding simply that, where an injurious growth in the body politic manifests itself, it is the root, or roots, of this that must be sought for and eradicated, not the surface tinkered, or gilded, or decently concealed; and that the eradication is to be done, not indeed without regard, but without too deterrent regard, for collateral disturbances that may ensue in the total organism. The sound parts, he maintains, will live and hold their own, if the true aim of the reform be conscientiously kept in view. It was as a Radical of this second kind that Althorp acted; and his Radicalism was all the more impressive because no man could be, by temperament and character, by habits of life and of thought, more deeply rooted in true English soil.

Encouraged overmuch by their success in the affair of the Duke of York, Whitbread's party proceeded to follow it up by moving for the appointment of a committee of inquiry into the existence of any corrupt practices in the disposal of offices in any department of the State. Here they had plainly overshot the mark. So indefinite a commission might have opened the way to more abuses than it suppressed. The motion was rejected by 178 to 30; the alienation of the Whigs was increased, and the Radicals lost ground with the country. Their next decided move was not till three years later, when, in 1812, they protested against the reinstatement of the Duke of York, but were again in a small minority. Althorp took part in this debate, but ineffectively. He had hardly spoken at all since his maiden speech of three years before, and it now seemed very unlikely that so unpractised and unskilled a speaker should ever take a leading part in Parliamentary politics. But though depressed by the defeat of this protest—a defeat which he thought a pernicious truckling to Court influence and a blow to honest administration—he was not silenced or discouraged on his own account. His taking part in debate depended not on his estimate of his own chance of personal display or aggrandizement, but on whether he thought his interference needful for the public weal. When the shoemakers of Northampton complained of a new tax on leather, he took up their case. It happened that Brougham, then a new member, was doing the same for the shoemakers of Stafford, and, with his usual love of the first place, he insisted on moving the rejection of the tax, leaving it to Althorp to second the motion. Brougham, like an advocate, tried to show the country squires with whom the House abounded how the tax would injure landowners; Althorp insisted on what was filling his own mind—the hardship threatened to the artisan and the labourer. On the other hand, when opposing as needless an extension of the local magistrates' powers in certain districts where rioting had occurred, he refused to join in the cry raised by some against the magistracy, expressly stating that his opposition was not grounded on fear of an abuse of the proposed powers. On these occasions, as well as on most others, he was in a minority; and when, in 1815, Whitbread died by his own hand, his mind having broken down under excess of work, his Radical followers became of less significance than ever. Their time was not yet come. The eyes of England were fixed, not on the benches of Westminster, but on the battlefields of Spain, of Russia, and of Flanders, fascinated by the mighty conflict begun at Torres Vedras and achieved at Waterloo. Before setting their house in order within, men must first make sure that it stands firm against the storm without.

CHAPTER III.

MARRIAGE AND BEREAVEMENT—LEADERSHIP OF THE LIBERAL OPPOSITION.

It is refreshing to know that these years of Parliamentary effacement, or at least insignificance, were filled with interest and delight in Althorp's private life. The stagnation in politics gave him leisure for occupations which he immeasurably preferred—occupations of the country and of home. He was fond of many manly exercises. When he was in town he kept himself in health and spirits by some of such as were available there. To the unsurpassed exercise of boxing he was ardently devoted, and attained great proficiency in it. We do not hear of his fencing. He kept up rackets, which he had learned at Harrow, but there seems to be no evidence that he proceeded to the more elaborate and nobler game of tennis. His chief passion, however, was for field-sports, and especially hunting. His seat was not very good, and he had frequent falls, sometimes dislocating his shoulder; nor was he ever a first-rate shot, though he greatly enjoyed shooting, and even kept a record of the game he killed or missed. But his greatest pleasure, he once said, was "to see sporting dogs hunt." He had become, like his father and grandfather, master of the Pytchley hounds, and that famous hunt was never more famous than under his charge. He justified what might have seemed an extravagant absorption in an amusement, by turning it to the best account as a means to draw closer all the ties of good-fellowship uniting various classes of the neighbourhood. Many years afterwards he would say that no other experience had taught him more of human nature. In later life he gave up hunting, and concentrated his energies, when he was in the country, on the improvement of agriculture and stock-breeding. For some years, however, about this time his dominant aim in life seemed to be to show the midland shires an ideal master of fox-hounds.

In his thirty-second year a higher and still more absorbing interest supervened; the interest of love and marriage. On the 14th of April, 1814, he married Esther, only child of Mr. Acklom, of

Wiseton Hall, Nottinghamshire—a girl some ten years younger than himself; and their union was profoundly happy. For the next four years neither sport nor politics was allowed to interrupt for long his delight in the companionship of his wife. It was the increasingly gloomy state of the country, the troubles of the dark and distressful years so disappointingly succeeding the Peace of 1815, that drove him back to his disinterested, and for a long time thankless, political labours. Throughout the session of 1818 he was constant in his censure of the reactionary and apathetic government of Sidmouth, Castlereagh, and Eldon, speaking much oftener than he had ever done before, and very much oftener than he could have forced himself to do unless under the conviction of imperative duty. Now that the war was victoriously ended, patriotic Liberals were no longer "muzzled" by fear of embarrassing the Government abroad if they insisted on reforms at home. When Parliament was prorogued in May, with a view to its dissolution that summer, Althorp looked for another golden interval of domestic joy. But that joy was now to end for him irrecoverably on earth. On the 11th of June, 1818, his wife died in childbirth, and the child with her. Thus at the same time perished his hope of the anxious but incomparable delights of fatherhood, which he was altogether fitted to enjoy. His house was left to him doubly desolate, and the anguish of his loss plunged him into a gloom and numbness from which for many months it seemed that no call could rouse him. Only his growing sensitiveness to the troubles of his countrymen gradually led him back to move again in a world where henceforth his pleasures must be of some austerer and less profound a kind. "The edge of his grief," says his friend and biographer, "was in some degree dulled by the efforts he made in discharge of what he conceived to be his duty. He thought that, if he could only combine hard work with retirement, he might succeed in bearing the burden of life with cheerfulness."

Hard work he was to have in plenty, but retirement, until the great task of his life was done, was to become less and less possible to him. While Parliament sat, he almost matched the Speaker in the regularity of his attendance at the House ; but outside it he saw hardly any one, burying himself in studies of political economy and of constitutional history and law. In the recess he continued these studies more uninterruptedly. He was missed at the covert-side and in the stubble; his hospitable house was void of guests; he only mixed with men to fulfil the graver duties of his place. In Parliament he chiefly busied himself with law reforms, which were greatly needed, but, from being unconnected with party politics, were then, as always, to most politicians totally unattractive.

After Romilly's death in 1818, Mackintosh took up his contest for reform of the criminal law. It was to another department of legal reform that Althorp especially applied himself. Under great difficulties and discouragement, and with labour which seemed altogether disproportioned to the result, he strove to procure an amendment of the laws relating to insolvent debtors, and to the recovery of small debts. On the former matter, after much thwarted toil as chairman of a committee, and then in charge of a Bill founded on the committee's report, he procured the establishment of a bankruptcy court of three judges, and at least diminished the scandalous ease with which fraudulent or negligent debtors had escaped the just consequences of their insolvency. One of the chief difficulties was made by the objection of the House of Lords to allow real estate to be made liable for the debts of an insolvent proprietor. When he had got this Act passed, he went on to bring in a Bill to facilitate the recovery of small debts by that very establishment of local courts which a quarter of a century later was accomplished with so great and beneficial an effect on the administration of justice. But almost all the lawyers were against him, and scouted not only the main provision of the Bill, but also the clause by which a simple statement of the cause of action was to take the place of the cumbrous and complicated pleadings then required. And when, in a fresh attempt in another session, he added a new clause, enabling the plaintiff and defendant to give evidence, this was no less fiercely denounced again by the authorities of the Bench and Bar. Yet both these innovations have now been accepted and approved by laymen and lawyers alike. Four times, in the four several sessions of 1821, 1823, 1824, and 1825, did Althorp bring in his Bill, each year with carefully considered variations; four times it was thwarted by professional and party narrowness, or worse.*

* Copley, afterwards Lord Lyndhurst, had given his adherence to the measure, when he found that Eldon, from whom he looked for promotion, was strongly against it. Copley then had the unscrupulous effrontery to turn round and oppose it by his speech and vote.

Even when he had converted Peel, in Peel's hands also a like Bill failed to pass.

Not till the County Courts Act of 1846 was passed did Althorp's patience and perseverance ultimately bear fruit; but he had sown the seeds of the public conviction which finally carried this reform, of inestimable value to the middle classes and to the poor. In Peel's words, "it was through Lord Althorp's perseverance that those inquiries were instituted that established the fact, not very creditable to the law of England, that there exists no remedy of which a prudent man can avail himself for the recovery of small debts." It is no slight credit to Althorp's insight and grasp of mind, as well as to his public spirit, that he may fairly be classed, as he has been by a legal writer, with Bentham himself as having been "in legal reform far in advance of his age." Nor could there well be a more impressive instance than the history of this matter toward proving that, with all due regard for the authority of legal experience, it is impossible to trust to professional initiative, or even sometimes to professional help, in the accomplishment of legal reforms.

To go back to 1819, in that year we find Althorp protesting against the Act carried by the

Tory ministry for the suppression of political meetings—an Act which was the effect of the excitement caused by the blundering mishap at Manchester, which went by the popular name of the Peterloo Massacre. That this protest was no demagogic bid for popularity is proved—if proof were needed—by his supporting the ministry in suppressing the nightly drills of the disaffected, and in all measures which might reasonably be held needful for the prevention of violence and outrage. The country had been in real and growing distress ever since the end of the war. It has been lately stated by the eminent statistician, Mr. Giffen, that in the last three centuries the years 1812–1822 formed, in his belief, the only decade in which there has been no material progress in this country. When in 1820 trade and manufactures began somewhat to improve, the price of corn fell throughout Europe, and the agricultural classes in England were in terror of ruin. And this was notwithstanding the Corn Law of 1815, which had yielded to the landowners the monopoly they clamoured for, and had sacrificed, it may be said, the interests of all other classes of the community to the interests concerned with the cultivation of land. Yet these interests also were now found to be in the gravest peril. A committee on the Corn Laws was appointed in the session of 1821, and Althorp was a member of it. It was sharply divided in opinion, and he took the side of Huskisson and Ricardo against the Protectionist members of the committee. After many disputatious meetings, the Protectionists at last ceased to attend a committee where their fallacies were refuted, and thus left it to Huskisson and his adherents to draw up the report, which was a powerful argument against the "interference, by protection or prohibition, with the application of capital in any branch of industry." Althorp was the only member for an agricultural constituency who voted for the report. It was not accepted by the Tory majority of the House, and the seceding members of the committee clamoured against the effect of their own secession. The committee was revived, on the understanding that it was not to displease the landowners. Huskisson resigned, and Castlereagh took his place, to prove himself, to the general surprise, a restraining influence on the Protectionist majority. The lame result of the whole matter was a new report, recommending a loan to distressed districts, the total exclusion of foreign corn under 70s. a quarter, and a sliding scale of duties, from 15s. to 10s., until the price should reach 80s. This was adopted by the Government, and embodied in an enactment, but without real benefit to English agriculture. The affair is mainly noticeable here as showing Althorp's detachment from the prejudices of his class, though he is not to be credited at this date with the more complete acceptance of the principles of Free Trade which he announced in the later years of his life.

Amid the various backwaters and eddies of its perplexed course, the stream had already begun to gather strength, which was to sweep away so many of the old barriers before another decade had well passed. Indications of a coming change began to multiply, though obscured by the details of party organization. After Castlereagh's suicide, in July, 1822, Canning took his place at the Foreign Office. The new foreign policy which made England again an effective Liberal influence in Europe was not the only change in this sense, though it was the most marked and remarkable. Huskisson, the Free-trader, was invited by Lord Liverpool to join the Cabinet as President of the Board of Trade. Robinson (afterwards Lord Goderich), who to a great extent shared Huskisson's views, became Chancellor of the Exchequer and the financial optimism which gained him the name of "Prosperity Robinson" seemed for a time justified by the extension of manufacturing industries, caused mainly by the development of mechanical invention. The enormous load of taxation was lightened, though still obviously grievous and crushing when considered in relation to the numbers and resources of the population at that time. The Navigation Laws were relaxed, and other approaches were made toward the general liberation of commerce from restraint. But much of this was done with very grudging support, or even against opposition, of the more unbending Tories; and the ministry came to lean more and more on the support of the Whigs.

In April, 1827, Liverpool was struck down by illness, and Canning at last became Prime Minister. Canning advanced the negotiations with the Opposition to a much further stage. He offered to form a coalition Cabinet to the extent of including in it three of the Whig leaders; and this offer took effect in the admission of Tierney, who had a somewhat indefinite pretension to lead the Opposition in the Commons, together with Lords Lansdowne and Holland. There were conditions, however, of the compact which condemned it in Althorp's eyes. The great questions on which his party had taken their stand—Parliamentary Reform, Catholic Emancipation, and the Repeal of the Test and Corporation Acts—were to be shirked and shelved, with no promise of future attempt to settle them. On this main ground, besides the inadequate proportion of the new element in the Cabinet, Althorp did his best to oppose the coalition. The opposite view was taken, not only by many of the most influential old Whigs, but also by many Radicals, including Burdett and Brougham; Brougham, indeed, was as much the author of the project of coalition as Canning was. But the event showed that Althorp had been right. Not that he attempted to justify his warning by damaging the new ministry; on the contrary, when the step had once been taken, he formally declared his acceptance of it, and loyally did his best to make the experiment a success. His object was not to prove himself right, but to take care how, while parties wrangled, his country should suffer least. He would not join in the fierce attacks of Grey and Ellenborough on the delusive coalition. He consented to serve on the Finance Committee, proposed by Canning and appointed after Canning's death by Goderich, who now became head of the Administration. Strangely enough, however, this step was the occasion, though not the cause, of the dissolution of the ministry. The chairmanship of the committee was offered to Althorp by Huskisson without consulting Herries, the Tory Chancellor of the Exchequer who had succeeded Goderich; and though Althorp was perfectly ready to give up the chair—and did give it up very shortly —Herries made this a ground for leaving the ministry. The disagreements, of which this was only one symptom, became intolerable; Goderich resigned, and the coalition Government fell to pieces.

In January, 1828, the Duke of Wellington became Prime Minister, and formed a Cabinet from which the Whig contingent had disappeared. But Canning's followers were represented by Huskisson, Grant, Lamb (afterwards Lord Melbourne), and Lords Palmerston and Dudley; and in Canning's followers the Liberal spirit of Canning still lived. Peel, though he could not strictly be classed as a "Canningite," had been Canning's colleague and supporter, and was too much of a statesman to be merely obstructive even then. Nor must the great duke himself ever be thus stigmatized. His principle was simply to make the most and best of things as they were and had been, when his country's right hand and his own had wrought marvellous things. He was loth that England should put on armour that she had not proved. It was this that made him a determined opponent of the reform of Parliament. But he had no love, as Lord Eldon and some Tories had, of maintaining privileges or disabilities for their own sake, though he might fear that things he loved and prized might fall with them if they fell. Of this he gave good proof in the first year of his premiership. In the session of 1828, Lord John Russell carried in the Commons a Bill repealing the Test and Corporation Acts, by which Protestant Dissenters had hitherto been, professedly at least, excluded from holding municipal and other offices; and beneath the shield of Wellington's authority the Bill was suffered to pass the Lords.

After this, it was manifest that the removal of Roman Catholic disabilities also must be only a matter of time. Catholics had long been in enjoyment of the suffrage, and posts in the army and navy were open to them, but they could not sit in Parliament, administer justice, or hold state or municipal offices. This was a grievance of the whole kingdom, but especially in Ireland. The Union of 1800 had been effected mainly for two great and worthy purposes—the security of the country against foreign aggression, and the protection of the Roman Catholic majority against the ascendency of the Protestant minority. While the Catholic disabilities were maintained, the second object could not be said to have been carried out, or the pledges of the Union to have been redeemed. To their redemption there had been one chief obstacle before, King George the Third, and there was one chief obstacle now, King George the Fourth. He was, indeed, backed by the House of Lords, but without his reciprocal backing the Lords would almost certainly have given way. He had withstood and thwarted Canning as his father had withstood and thwarted Pitt, but his resistance was now, at last, to yield to Wellington. For the moment, indeed, there seemed likely to be a reaction. In May, 1828, Huskisson resigned on the question of an isolated fragment of Parliamentary Reform—the disfranchisement of East Retford—and the Canningite members of the Cabinet quitted it with him. But any want of "pro-Catholic" pressure within the Government was more than compensated by an extraordinary pressure outside. The "Catholic Committee" and O'Connell saw that the long-delayed justice was now about to be done, and the instinct of the "Great Agitator" seized on the occasion. He presented himself as a candidate for the county of Clare, and was triumphantly elected. Great excitement, with continual danger of hostile collisions with Orangemen, was kept up for many months in Ireland. In March, 1829, the Emancipation Bill was brought in by Peel in the Commons, and on the last day of the month it passed the third reading by a majority of 173. In ten days more it had passed in the House of Lords, thanks to Wellington's authority, by a majority of 105; and on the 13th of April it received the royal assent. The evil done by the two kings was to live after them, but at least their harmful action in this matter was now for ever at an end. Only once more, and that transiently and almost innocuously, was the Crown to be found obstructing a reform, and the nation injured by the obstacle of its single will. That was when William the Fourth drew back for a few days at the crisis of the struggle for the Reform Bill; and never since then has any such incident marred the constitutional relations of sovereign and people to each other.

It need hardly be said that Althorp, who in 1824 had moved for a committee on the condition of Ireland, gave his warmest support to the Government in removing the Catholic disabilities. Nor did he join or countenance the taunts launched occasionally from both sides of the House at the ministry on account of their conduct in this matter. Some complained that they had set a dangerous example by seeming to give way before the alarm of insurrection. It was true that one of the chief circumstances influencing Wellington had been the grave peril of civil war; and it was worthy of the great soldier's wisdom and humanity to take that peril into account. None could foretell whether forcible control of the Catholic agitation, if found needful, would be forcibly resisted or not. It might, indeed, have happened that, when they saw the arm of England raised to strike in earnest, the agitators would have shrunk back, and the agitation collapsed. So it came to pass in 1843, when, at the height of a still more formidable-seeming agitation for Repeal, the Government intervened to forbid the Clontarf meeting, and O'Connell and the vast and surging hosts of the Repealers went quietly back to their own homes. But in 1829 the resistance of the Roman Catholics seemed at least as probable as their submission; and though Wellington could not yet recognize in Emancipation a plain requisite of justice, he could see, especially after the abrogation of the Test and Corporation Acts, that it stood on a very different footing from Repeal of the Union, and that the question was not worth the bloody subjugation of his fellow-citizens, of whom so many, as he feelingly reminded the Lords, had fought and bled under his own command for the honour of the British flag.

Some detractors, again, complained of the Administration on the charge of having adopted, for the sake of retaining office, an interested and unprincipled change of policy. But the position of the Catholic question afforded no sound warrant for such a charge. Tory governments had always been divided on that question, and their most eminent chiefs, Pitt and Canning, had been in favour of the Catholic claims, and had resigned office when they failed to persuade the king to yield. Peel had, in private at least, shown some inclination to the concession in 1824. It had been generally considered, whether erroneously or not, on the Tory side at least, as a question of expediency, as a matter on which the advantages and disadvantages must be balanced against each other—the dangers of Catholic discontent on the one hand, and the dangers of encroachment on the Established Church on the other. There was no party or group in Parliament whose votes could be secured for general support of the Government by a change of policy on this point. The Roman Catholics were not represented in Parliament; those who had all along advocated their claims would, of course, not feel bound in any way to further adherence to the Ministry when the measure had once been passed; indeed, many of the Opposition would resent the appropriation by Tories of what might be held to be a Whig measure. On the other hand, it would have been useless for the Tories to resign, with a view to the Whigs taking office to pass the Bill, for there was then no apparent prospect that the Whigs could possibly have a majority in the House of Commons, or in the country. Althorp was not the man to overlook a step of questionable integrity; and had there been anything discreditable in the ministerial measure, it could no more have escaped his censure in the House of Commons than it could have obtained the sanction of Wellington in the Cabinet.

This generous attitude toward ministers is not, perhaps, a very usual attitude in one who has claims to a leading place in an Opposition; but Althorp's party could not fail to see that if he preferred "measures to men," this did not mean that he affected an indifference to party ties, or was incompetent to party leadership. It has been well said that the man who begins by preferring his party to his country will end by preferring himself to both. Conversely, the man who veritably prefers his country to his party will also prefer his party to himself. He will not suffer himself to be dragged helplessly in party chains, but neither will he wantonly break up his party to serve the opportunities of a selfish ambition, or the caprices of a headstrong will.

It was in May, 1830, that the sense of Althorp's qualifications for leadership found definite expression among the Liberal members of the House. The first half of the session of that year had left them still in a disorganized condition. The chief interest in the Commons had been in certain debates on questions of financial reform, and in these debates Althorp had distinguished himself by wisdom, boldness, and independence. In supporting a motion by Poulett Thomson for a committee on expenditure and taxation, he startled both sides of the House by advocating the imposition of an income tax—an impost till then regarded as justifiable only in time of war. The proposal found little support then, but in 1842 Peel's introduction of the tax was one of the economic reforms which established his fame, and since then no ministry has ever ventured to propose its abolition in the House of Commons. When some of the Radicals joined with the Tory malcontents in demanding a depreciation of the currency, Althorp's speech in opposition to the demand was believed to have won many votes toward the large majority by which the House then supported the Government. In the same spirit he received the estimates with expressions of satisfaction, acknowledging them as on the whole, the best yet laid before the House. Those who took a more aggressive course did not succeed in carrying the House with them, and there was a general feeling both that the party had not made the most of its opportunities for improving its position in the country, and that the "friendly opposition" of Althorp to the Government had been the most judicious as well as the most honest policy in the circumstances. The result was a meeting of Liberal members in May, at which it was resolved formally to request him to act as their leader in the House. He was loth to be preferred to Brougham and Russell, but his reluctance was overcome. He was the leader who "least divided" the party of reform. It was understood now that Liberal members were not to take action against the ministry without his sanction. Under the appropriate name of "The Watchmen," he and four others undertook the task of careful attention to the proceedings of the Government, and of reporting on them as deserving opposition or support.

On the 26th of June, 1830, the king died, and his brother, the Duke of Clarence, succeeded him as William the Fourth. The two last Georges had exercised influence of an obstructive kind in politics, and the general belief that William would be differently disposed, contributed, whether with constitutional propriety or not, to the growing hopes of the reformers.

On the 24th of July Parliament was dissolved, and the writs were made returnable on the 14th of September.

CHAPTER IV.

ACCEPTANCE OF OFFICE AND LEADERSHIP OF THE HOUSE OF COMMONS.

The general election of 1830 gave only a very partial indication of the magnitude of the issues that were to be decided in the next two years. In some constituencies the contest was on the question of Parliamentary Reform, but in many it was influenced more by other matters, and, of course, often by personal popularities. Althorp himself was again returned for his own county of Northamptonshire without opposition. That which seems to have turned the scale in the elections as a whole was not, as yet, any general or enthusiastic desire of Liberal measures, but the discontent of the more uncompromising Tories with the Acts of religious emancipation passed by Wellington's Government. These Tories stood sullenly aloof, or even opposed the ministerial candidates; and when the House of Commons assembled on the 2nd of November, it became apparent that the ministry must fall. Within a fortnight a motion from the Opposition side to refer the Civil List to a select committee was carried by a majority of twenty-nine. Next day, the 16th of the month, the duke resigned, and a Liberal ministry was called to office.

In the formation of the new Government there could be little doubt that the place of Prime Minister fell naturally to the venerable Earl Grey, the last eminent survivor of the following of Fox and Grenville, and distinguished by nearly half a century of honourable exile from all hope of place and power. But not only was Lord Grey an old man in his sixty-seventh year, who had three years before spoken of his political career as finished, but also by his peerage he was excluded from the House of Commons, where the forthcoming Liberal measures were to be introduced, and their fate virtually decided. The first question, therefore, and the most imperative, that presented itself to him in forming a ministry was the question of who was to be the leader of the House of Commons. There were several men of great ability who seemed to have claims to that post. The ablest and historically most conspicuous members on the Liberal side were Henry Brougham, Lord Palmerston, Lord John Russell, Edward Stanley, and Macaulay. Macaulay, a young man of thirty and a new member, was, of course, out of the question, and the same objection of youth applied to Stanley and Russell. Palmerston was one of the Canningite section of the Liberal party, and had only lately become an adherent of Parliamentary Reform. It was, indeed, with great reluctance and distaste that Grey accepted the accession of the Canningites to his party and Government. By far the most active and prominent, the most brilliant and the most widely known member of the late Liberal Opposition, was Henry Brougham, a man of marvellous versatility, of indefatigable energy, of copious and ardent eloquence, of unequalled celebrity at that moment in the political world. Had the posts in that memorable ministry been allotted according to the principles which have too often tended to prevail in this country, there can hardly be a doubt that the most important post, the leadership of the House of Commons, would have been assigned to Brougham. There can hardly be any less doubt that such assignment would have been a fatal mistake. The country would to its cost have realized then, as it has perhaps realized since, how fluency, versatility, and restless energy may be dangerously dissociated from comprehensive thought, patriotic sincerity, and statesmanlike wisdom. Brougham's mental gifts were of a most extraordinary, though not of the very highest, kind; and perhaps his countrymen, in disappointment at the failure of his exceeding early promise, have been disposed to err on the side of severity in their judgment of him. But, at any rate, his whole career made it plainly manifest that he had neither the tact, nor the straightforwardness, nor the self-control, nor the self-forgetfulness, which were required for the arduous and delicate task of conducting the great struggle of that epoch to a peaceful victory.

Passing over these brilliant names, Lord Grey's choice fell unerringly and, it would seem, unhesitatingly, on Lord Althorp. The position to which we have seen that Althorp had been already elected by a group of Liberal members of the Opposition in the spring of that year, had of course by no means given him a conclusive claim to his new honours. The number of that group he himself estimates (in a letter, written in March, to Grey) at exactly forty. "The principle of our junction," he says, "is to extend only to measures of retrenchment and reduction of taxes. On other points we are to continue as disunited as ever."

A leadership of this kind, which Althorp made a post of friendly criticism of the Wellington Government, was a very different thing from the leadership in the arduous and terribly responsible enterprise of conducting a political campaign in a cause which was to stir the country to its depths, to rouse against itself the forces of enthroned and threatened privilege, and boldly to avow that nothing less than a great organic constitutional change was virtually its aim. But Lord Grey believed that the modest and uneloquent Althorp was the man to pilot the vessel of the State through that stormy and dangerous strait of sea; and the event proved that this belief was right. Grey's confidence in Althorp went even beyond this point. Mistrusting the powers of his own old age, and also his capacity of acting harmoniously with the Canningites introduced into the Whig ministry, he earnestly pressed Althorp to take the place of Prime Minister instead of himself. This proposal Althorp absolutely and decisively refused. Indeed, he only accepted the leadership of the House of Commons and Chancellorship of the Exchequer with great reluctance, and after repeated assurance from Lord Grey that he was indispensable to his party's cause.

It is noticeable and contrastedly characteristic (and there is nothing invidious in recalling the incident) that Palmerston, not knowing Grey's choice, actually proposed himself to him for the leadership in the Commons; but on hearing from his chief that the post was to be Althorp's, he at once declared his complete satisfaction. Nor did Brougham, though by no means satisfied with the Great Seal as a substitute for the leadership, show any of the feeling toward Althorp which might have been feared from a man of his temperament toward a supplanting rival. Through all differences and disputes with the Cabinet as a whole, or with the members of it, Brougham never seems to have quarrelled with Althorp, and till late in the life of the latter he maintained a cordial friendship and correspondence with him.

To Palmerston was allotted the Foreign Office, his most congenial and henceforth familiar sphere. The Cabinet included three other Canningite members—Melbourne, Goderich, and Charles Grant. Russell and Stanley remained for the present, but not for long, outside the Cabinet.

The selection of Althorp as leader of the House gave additional emphasis to the stipulation made by the prime minister with the king, that if he was to accept the government of the country, it could only be on condition that the reform of Parliamentary representation was to be recognized as the first work to be undertaken. It was known that by Althorp, fully as much as by his chief, the achievement of Reform was cherished as the main purpose of his political life. He regarded it, not indeed as a panacea for social ills, but as an indispensable preliminary to their alleviation, as well as a plain piece of justice. Modest and slow in forming and expressing an opinion on most points of policy, he had concentrated his enthusiasm on this, on which he saw his way with perfect clearness; and one deliberate and reasoned enthusiasm is more potent than ten of hasty and emotional growth. Men of this kind were needed to lead the way, if the thing was to be done at all. It must not be forgotten that until a project of Reform was actually before the country in a tangible shape, there was comparatively little public interest in the matter. There was much discontent and much misery among the poor, but it did not express itself habitually or principally in a demand for an extended or redistributed suffrage. In keeping alive the tradition that Parliamentary Reform was an indispensable means toward other reforms, the public men of the Whig party did that on which they may fairly rest one of their chief claims to our respect and gratitude. Reform was no suggestion of late years. It had been projected by the elder Pitt and other statesmen in the latter part of the eighteenth century. It is curious to note that the notion for a committee to inquire into the representation with a view to Reform, which was made in the House of Commons by the younger Pitt in 1782, was only thrown out by a majority of twenty (161 to 141). Reform never came so near again to accomplishment until its final victory just half a century later. It need hardly be said that in that half-century the inequalities of representation had enormously increased. There were fifty-six English Parliamentary boroughs, each with a population of less than two thousand persons, and these fifty-six boroughs returned one hundred and eleven members. There were also thirty boroughs containing less than four thousand persons, which returned two members apiece. Here lay the first great grievance to be redressed. Most of these hundred and seventy-one seats were for boroughs of the "rotten" kind, of which so much was then heard; that is, they were simply and avowedly the property of individual rich men. Many of these men were Indian "nabobs," and others who had made large fortunes by commerce or speculation, but the greater part of the borough-owners were members of the House of Lords, who thus, by putting in their nominees, contrived practically to possess seats in both Houses at once. Herein lay the central and vital issue which made the Reform Act of 1832 a real revolution, a great and pregnant alteration of the balance of powers within the Commonwealth. Although for two centuries the main centre of the country's interest had lain in the House of Commons, yet the system of nomination boroughs had practically maintained an equality of power in the House of Lords.

The second great grievance in the eyes of the Reformers—the concomitant and complement of the first—was that the great manufacturing towns, which had sprung up or immensely increased in the last half-century throughout the northern and midland counties, were most of them not Parliamentary boroughs at all, and that their inhabitants were absolutely unrepresented except when they happened to have votes for the county. It is to be remembered that under the Protectorate of Oliver Cromwell some of these towns had been made boroughs, but had been deprived of their franchise after the Stuart Restoration, apparently with their own consent, or at least indifference. Since that time those towns, with many others which were then insignificant hamlets, or even spaces of unpeopled earth, had grown to be a great constituent element of the State, nourishing it with men and money, and now claiming loudly a voice in the deliberations of its representative assembly. By the side of these two main grievances the demand for a lowering of the property qualification for the franchise, so as to include in this way also a larger number of voters, was at this epoch comparatively unemphatic; except in Scotland, where the franchise in counties was incredibly limited, and in boroughs was greatly abused by the close corporations possessing it. The ten-pound franchise ultimately established by the coming Act seems on the whole to have satisfied this demand so far as it existed; but such demand played a far less prominent part at this epoch than in the subsequent Reforms of 1867 and 1885.

At the beginning of the year 1831 the preponderance of forces influencing public opinion and the course of events was, as the issue proved, in favour of a measure of organic Reform. But that preponderance was by no means either obvious or overwhelming. Every favourable influence had its limitation and counteraction. The new ministry enjoyed at present the support of a Parliamentary majority and of the king. But the Parliamentary majority included, as we have seen, an element of merely malcontent Tories, whose quarrel with the Wellington Government had been, not that it reformed too little, but that it reformed too much. The king was an uncertain ally; he very soon showed an inconvenient sensitiveness about the Civil List, and he was subject to Court influences which were sure to be hostile to any comprehensive political change. The Canningites had joined the Reformers, but by Grey and some other Liberals they were still regarded with very imperfect trust.

On the other hand, the prevailing economic distress, which showed itself in the disastrous form of rick-burning, had sharpened the vague demand of the people for some sweeping change which might be a step towards the relief of their miseries, though the demand had not yet taken definite shape in support of Parliamentary Reform. It was more likely at first to be a demand for administrative economies, and this might as easily prove an embarrassment as a help to the new ministry. The Duke of Wellington and his Cabinet, whatever their defects in other points, had in this matter been faithful stewards of the national estate, and almost all the retrenchments then possible in expenditure and reductions of taxation had been already made in the two years and three-quarters during which the duke had been in power. He himself considered that he had lost support among his party fully as much by his large sacrifice of patronage as by his removal of religious disabilities. His successors, and Althorp conspicuously, had always acknowledged his good service in the matter of retrenchment, and saw that if expectations of further economies were to be excited in the country, such expectations would very probably lead to serious disappointment among the people, and to discredit of the new ministry.

The influences to be taken into account were not confined to the United Kingdom. The successful and rapid revolution in France of the three days of July, 1830, had had a sympathetic effect in this country, which on the whole encouraged and strengthened the movement for Reform. The change of the French dynasty had been effected with little bloodshed or lawlessness, and the new settlement appeared to promise a decided restraint of arbitrary privilege and a firmer establishment of constitutional order. Yet here again the effect in this country was not wholly in favour of the Reformers. It was argued by some that the late revolution in France, however salutary, had been effected by force, and that, in view of the widely spread distress and discontent in England, of which the rick-burning and other sporadic disorders were symptoms, the communication of a revolutionary spirit from the Continent might push forward political agitation over the verge of social anarchy. The initiation of large and exciting changes might thus be a perilous letting out of waters. Arguments of such a kind, reinforcing the old objections to Reform, did at this time unquestionably influence no less a mind than that of Peel. Notwithstanding the great qualities, including patience, firmness, and clear sight, which he repeatedly showed as a statesman and administrator, Peel seems to have been justly deemed by many who knew him to be constitutionally liable to "political panic." It was he who was mainly responsible for the ministerial decision which, in vague fear of riot, postponed the king's visit to the City and the State banquet of November 9, 1830—a decision only transiently injurious to the country, but fatal to the ministry that adopted it. Before this he had said in private that he believed that the monarchy could not last more than some five or six years. And if Peel's forebodings were dark, it is plain that the forebodings of many men with less knowledge than he had of the national character must have been darker still, and must have made them shrink in no pretended fear from the untravelled way. To such fears the Reformers, of course, replied that only by a truer representation of the people could their wants and grievances be discovered and removed, and that the constitution would be more firmly established on a broader base. But it was not merely on the immediate present that the objectors grounded their fears, nor were those fears confined to men whose opinions could be called exaggerated or extreme. No public man who had hitherto felt the responsibility of office had shown himself more sensible of the need of far-reaching changes, of the breaking down of many monopolies and privileges, than the Free-trader and Emancipationist Huskisson. He was in favour of a partial Reform, and his support of the transference of the franchise from East Retford to Birmingham had even been the occasion of his resignation of his seat in the Cabinet. In the early part of 1830 he supported Russell's Bill for enfranchising Birmingham, Manchester, and Leeds. But he took that opportunity to declare his unabated antagonism to any measure of Reform "founded on a general revision, reconstruction, and remodelling of our present constitution. He conceived that if such an extensive Reform were effected, they might go on for two or three sessions in good and easy times, and such a reformed Parliament might adapt itself to our mode of government and the ordinary concerns of the country; but if such an extensive change were effected in the constitution of Parliament, sure he was that whenever an occasion arose of great popular excitement or reaction, the consequence would be a total subversion of our constitution, followed by complete confusion and anarchy, terminating first in the tyranny of a fierce democracy, and then in that of a military despotism, those two great calamities maintaining that natural order of succession which they had always been hitherto seen to observe. Regarding the present system as a whole, he was opposed to any material change in it."

Huskisson was now gone, killed in the first railway accident at the opening of the first railway in September, 1830; but the convictions he had expressed lived on in the minds of his old colleagues, and of many men outside Parliament who had welcomed his administrative improvements. Behind their honest caution was a mass of merely selfish conservatism, clinging blindly to the irresponsible possession of power, which found expression in the notorious claim of the Duke of Newcastle to "do what he would with his own." All such naked assertions of private property in political trusts did indeed make Reform more ultimately inevitable and irresistible, but they also were symptoms of the tenacious antagonism it would have to overcome. On the whole survey of the situation we see, therefore, that the opening of the year 1831 gave the Reformers good hope, but no certain promise, of success; and the fulfilment of that hope could be earned only by clear heads and stout hearts. The leaders could already stand the test, but their followers needed the sifting of further trial. The House of Commons which placed the new ministry in power was not the House destined to decree the great Act of Reform.

CHAPTER V.

THE FIRST REFORM BILL.

PARLIAMENT reassembled, after the Christmas adjournment, on the 3rd of February, 1831; and Althorp immediately announced in the Commons that a Bill for the reform of Parliamentary representation would be brought forward on the 1st of March. The intervening month was occupied by the discussion of less momentous measures, including, however, the Budget, which Althorp, as Chancellor of the Exchequer, had to prepare and introduce. Without containing any very imposing rearrangements of taxation, this Budget seems to have been reasonable and creditable enough, not unworthy of a successor of Huskisson and a predecessor of Peel. It was not permitted to Althorp to carry out his favourite project of an income-tax; in this matter he was still too much in advance of his time. But whatever, short of this, could be done to shift the burden of taxation from the poorer classes to the richer, and to liberate and encourage important industries, this he was still bent on doing. The Budget proposed to lower or repeal the duties on glass, printed calicoes, candles, coals, timber, tobacco (on which the duty was to be reduced by half); and no less than one hundred and sixty-three small but vexatious duties were swept away. The stamp duty on newspapers was to be less by half. Altogether the diminution of taxation was to be a little over four millions. Compensation was to be effected by reducing or abolishing the payment of two hundred and sixty offices, by imposition or equalization of a few new import and export duties, chiefly by a tax on transfers of real and funded property. The really weakest point of the Budget was a duty (though but a low one) to be laid on raw cotton, from which half a million was to be expected. But the proposal which aroused the strongest opposition was that of the tax on transfers of funded property. To this opposition, backed by an outcry in the City, the Cabinet yielded, though Althorp wished to stand firm on this point, believing that the opinion of financiers would come round to his. The tax was given up; and as it had been counted on to supply nearly a million and a quarter, its withdrawal involved the abandonment of the promised remissions on glass and tobacco. The mutilated Budget looked insignificant, and all this was somewhat to the disadvantage of the ministry and their Chancellor of the Exchequer. They had already caused some disappointment the week before by their settlement of the Civil List. Concessions in the matter of maintaining pensions had to be made to the king, whose goodwill it was important to retain with a view to more momentous issues near at hand. Some important checks and limitations of the Civil List were introduced, but not enough to satisfy the stricter economists. Great pressure was put on Althorp to persuade him to restrictions which he did himself desire to effect; but having made up his mind as to the compromise which he thought right for the present, and having given his word to the king, he stood doggedly to his plan. Nor did his credit with the House suffer, on the whole, for this. Jeffrey, who with other Edinburgh reviewers had lately entered Parliament, wrote of him in these days in a letter: "There is something to me quite delightful in his calm, clumsy, courageous, immutable probity and well-meaning, and it seems to have a charm with everybody."

The February of this year must have been as laborious a month as any ministry have ever undergone. While their financial measures had to be defended in debate, they were working under great pressure to prepare the Reform Bill for the appointed day. For this preparation a committee of four was appointed; these were Sir James Graham, Lord Durham, Lord Duncannon, and Lord John Russell. This committee reported on each section to Grey and Althorp, who then together moulded a corresponding proposal to lay before the whole Cabinet. Althorp's influence seems to have been employed throughout in strengthening and broadening the measures as much as possible. This he did on grounds both of justice and of expediency, for only a bold and broad scheme could arouse the enthusiasm in the country which he saw would be needed to carry through Reform.

The utmost secrecy as to the provisions of the Bill was anxiously observed by its framers; and this was no easy matter amidst the fervent curiosity of both friends and foes. It was not till the last week of February that the Bill was committed to the official Parliamentary draftsmen for embodiment in its final shape. But before then it had been necessary to have at least ten or twelve copies made for the use of members of the Cabinet. Some were made by a few clerks in the public offices, who honourably fulfilled their bond of secrecy; some by Lord Durham's wife and eldest child, the daughter and granddaughter of Grey. When the fateful first of March had come, the secret of the ministry was still their own.

The history of the next sixteen months of the successive acts of this great political drama is an oft-told tale. But as Althorp's part in it is the ground of his most signal claim to enduring honour, it must needs be told briefly here once more.

The introduction of the Bill had been entrusted to Lord John Russell, future Prime Minister of England, but at that time little known, and without a place in the Cabinet. He acquitted himself well. On the evening of the promised day his small spare form and pale determined face rose amid the thronged benches of the old House of Commons; and never, during more than two centuries of existence, had that historic building known a more memorable scene. Russell spoke for almost two hours, beginning with an exposition of the general plan and principles of the measure, and proceeding to its particular provisions. He kept to the latter part of his speech the famous schedules of the disfranchised boroughs. Sixty boroughs were to be politically annihilated, and one hundred and eight besides were to lose one seat. Member after member heard sentence passed on his constituency—the constituency generally, indeed, consisting of a single magnate—and political extinction threatened to its representative. But the sentences were impartially pronounced; the Bill was free from the stain of party intrigue. As in the States-General of France in 1789, so now, but with happier omen, the Liberal nobility came forward to sacrifice ancestral privileges to the common weal. The Russells and Cavendishes and their like were ready to maintain their traditional influence in the country without the aid of their host of nomination seats in Parliament. But the feeling which possessed both sides of the House as they listened to the audacious schedules, and the stirring appeal that followed them and closed the speech, was neither admiration nor resentment, but confounding and blank wonder. During the reading of the schedules there had been cheers, ironic laughter, and hostile cries hurled loudly and eagerly across the floor of the House. But during the peroration the minds of members were at comparative leisure to brood on their amazement, and it overpowered and held them dumb. When Russell sat down there was a deep silence, more significant than cheers. The House was absorbed in straining its mental gaze to imagine the new England which seemed foreshadowed in the startling words they had just heard.

It was believed by Brougham and others that if Peel and the Conservative leaders had simply refused to discuss the measure at all, on the ground of its extravagant and revolutionary character, the House would have rejected it on the first reading. It might have been so, or it might not; at any rate, this way of meeting the Bill was not attempted. As Russell's speech drew to its close, Peel buried his face in his hands, and sat as a man confounded, without attempt at reply. But Sir Robert Inglis, Peel's old supplanter at Oxford, rose to speak for some two hours against Reform of any kind; and the same line was taken by one or two of the less eminent Tory members. Meanwhile the lobbies were filled with excited groups, exclaiming, criticizing, eagerly inquiring and speculating, too distracted by surprise and by fear or hope to attend or contribute to regular and decorous debate. At last Althorp rose, and ended that sitting of the House with a speech wholly different from Russell's in kind, but the best possible supplement to it. He gravely and resolutely reasserted the purpose of the ministry, with their reasons for it, and for the means that they proposed, especially those which had weighed most with himself. His speech had the effect of making the House feel once more on firm ground, and in the presence of an unquestionable reality. As the members went homeward about midnight they felt that the time of declamation was over; that a great and definite enterprise was set before them which they must decide either to oppose or to achieve; and that the plan set forth that night embodied the deliberate and reasoned convictions of men who would not swerve from their resolve.

The Bill was read a first time without a division. On the second reading there were seven nights of eager and often eloquent debate. The most significant incident occurred in Peel's speech, and it was an incident of encouragement to the ministry. He had recovered from his first stupefaction, and spoke against the Bill with an oratorical vigour and elaboration worthy of himself and of the hour. But though he opposed the Bill, it was not with the uncompromising opposition which the majority of his party desired. When the words fell from his lips in which he seemed to admit that some concession must be made, that some reform of Parliamentary representation must be allowed, then the cheers of his followers abated ominously; and the extremest Tories spoke bitterly of him among themselves, as though they were feeling that a breach had been made in their defences, and were suspecting faint-heartedness, if not treachery, in their chief.

The division on the second reading was taken in the fullest house ever known. Six hundred and three members voted, making, with the Speaker and tellers, a House of six hundred and eight. Three hundred and two voted for the Bill, thus giving the Reformers a majority of one. It was a victory for the moment, but the numbers showed already that if the Bill was to be passed without mutilation it must be by another House of Commons than this. When the Bill was in committee a series of hostile amendments were moved by the Opposition, and more than once, and on important points, the ministry were now in a minority. The last of their defeats was on April 21, when an adjournment was carried against them by a majority of twelve. Then they made their decision, the most critical and momentous in the history of their Bill. Parliament must be dissolved, and the country appealed to for its judgment on the question of Reform.

The chief obstacle to this step was the king's aversion to it. When it had been talked of before, he had always shown the strongest disinclination to dissolve so young a Parliament, though he was equally indisposed to accept the resignations of his ministers. To us, at this day, it seems clear enough that a direct appeal to the country was the only solution of the crisis, especially as the reform of Parliament had not been proposed as the main question to the constituencies in the general election of the preceding autumn. But this principle was then less distinctly recognized, and there was also the strongest possible protest against a dissolution on the part of the Opposition and their supporters in the country. Fortunately, their antagonism overleaped itself. Lord Wharncliffe having failed to obtain an answer from Grey in the House of Lords as to whether a dissolution was intended, gave notice that he should next day move an address to the Crown remonstrating against such exercise of the prerogative. When the news of this notice came to the king, it found him, on the morning of the 22nd of April, in debate with Grey and two or three other ministers, who, after some hours of argument, were just beginning to prevail upon him to dissolve. He still hung back, when the tidings of proposed interference of the Lords with his prerogative kindled the smouldering fire of his will. He was in haste to be at the House, and the ministers sped his haste. Yet, before he could leave the palace in his state carriage, the peers had assembled at two o'clock in the afternoon, and Wharncliffe had risen to speak on his motion for the address. He was interrupted by the Duke of Richmond's calling on the peers to be seated in their places—an intimation of the coming of the king. Then followed cries and counter-cries of "Order!" with recriminations so fierce that Richmond moved that the standing order against offensive language be read; then above the clamour came the sudden thunder of the guns, announcing that the king was on his way. Still Wharncliffe persisted in reading through his address, and Mansfield rose to support it. The disorder increased; the peers shouted and yelled, and shook their fists in each other's faces. The cries of, "The king! the king!" were heard repeatedly across the tumult. Mansfield could be heard at intervals declaiming against ministers for "conspiring together against the safety of the State, and making the sovereign the instrument of his own destruction." While these last words were in their ears, the lords saw the doors behind the throne open; and Durham, as Lord Privy Seal, entered, bearing the crown. Then came the king himself, and the storm subsided sullenly, while the Commons were summoned from their House. The excitement there had been hardly less violent than in the Lords. Althorp, Peel, and Burdett had been all together struggling to be heard, and when Peel was called on by the Speaker, such words as could be heard from him only exasperated the disorder of the scene. At the royal summons some hundred members thronged to the House of Lords, with Althorp in triumph at their head. Then the king made his expected speech, and Parliament was dissolved.

CHAPTER VI.

THE REFORM ACT.

THE new general election proved conclusively that the cause of Reform was won with the electors; that the great majority of them were willing to share their privileges with a larger and more truly representative constituency. The general apathy which for so many years had disheartened the leaders of the movement was now at an end. The success of the ministry was not more marked in the boroughs than in the counties, where the Tories had expected most support. In Northamptonshire Althorp would readily have acquiesced in a division of the representation with the sitting Tory member; but the Liberals of the county insisted on running another candidate, Lord Milton, for the second place. They were justified by the result. Althorp headed the poll, and Milton obtained the second seat.

The new Parliament met on the 21st of June, and on the 24th Russell moved for leave to bring in a new Reform Bill, which was virtually the old. It was read the first time without debate, and the second reading was fixed for the 4th of July, before which date Scotch and Irish Reform Bills were also brought in. On the second reading there was a debate lasting three nights, in which Althorp again made one of the weightiest speeches delivered. Then the House divided, and the effect of the new elections was made plain. In a House of 598 the ministry had a majority of 136. On the 12th of July the House went into committee on the Bill. Now began a protracted struggle, which strained to the utmost the firmness, the skill, and above all the patience of the supporters of the Bill, and more especially of those of their leaders who were in charge of its conduct through the House. Every means of obstruction was resorted to by the Opposition, including an "all-night" sitting and many dilatory motions for adjournment. After a few weeks Russell's health gave way under the incessant strain, and then the management of the Bill devolved upon Althorp alone. The disfranchisement clauses, with their schedules of seats to be abolished, were naturally the field of the fiercest fights. The clause containing Schedule A virtually contained fifty-seven clauses, and each was contested to the uttermost. Against this indefatigable attack Althorp maintained an equally indefatigable defence. By unflinching industry he had mastered every detail, and the justification of every detail, of that elaborate and momentous scheme; and with unfailing temper and unfailing fairness he rose to argue and to reply, to explain and to defend, from evening to morning twilight of the wasted summer days. Debarred from his accustomed exercise, he traded, so to speak, on his accumulated stock of health, which he contrived to maintain by very careful and simple diet. Macaulay writes, in a letter to his sisters, of how Althorp had been describing to him his habit of life at this time. He used to go to his office after breakfast and remain there till nearly four o'clock. At four he dined, and would then go down to the House at five, and remain there till it rose, generally much after midnight. When he got home he would make his supper on a basin of arrowroot and a glass of sherry. It was not till the 30th of August that indisposition ever kept him from the House, and then it was only for two days. By some his fortitude and self-control might be misunderstood. Lord Stanhope says that he had attributed his calm demeanour to "sluggishness" of temperament, till he heard him say afterwards that during those months of sore trial it was well he never found a pistol by his bedside when he awoke, for it would have been hard to refrain from ending the physical and mental harassment of his life. Indeed, he told Sir John Hobhouse that he had taken the precaution of removing pistols from his room. Not till the 7th of September did the committee report, and then followed yet another fortnight of superfluous debate. On the 21st the Bill was read a third time by a majority of 109 in a House of 581. On the next day Althorp and Russell, at the head of some two hundred of the Commons, solemnly presented the Bill at the bar of the House of Lords. There it was in the hands of the men whose power it was to cut down and curb. It was hardly possible that they would yield as yet. The magnificent speeches of Grey and Brougham were delivered in vain, though of the latter Lord Holland declared that it surpassed the finest speeches of his uncle, Charles James Fox. For the second reading there were only 158 votes to 199, leaving a majority of 41 against the Bill. Had not the sense of the country been so emphatically declared in the late elections, this majority would probably have been much larger. As it was, the result of the division was received with but faint cheers, and the Tory lords were soon in disquietude and terror at their own audacity. But for the present they had given the challenge, and must abide by it.

The Commons lost no time in taking up the glove. The Bill had been rejected by the peers on the 7th of October. On the same day a meeting of the supporters of the ministry resolved that a vote of confidence in the Government should be moved in the House of Commons by Lord Ebrington on the 10th. There was a strong feeling of indignation and resentment, not only in the House but throughout the people; a feeling which it might become difficult to restrain within the rule of law.

Althorp's responsibilities became more burdensome and more critical than ever. At a Cabinet Council it was decided that he, and he only, should speak for the Government in the coming debate on Ebrington's motion. On the morning of the 10th he wrote to his father—

"The speech I have to make to-night is terrific; one word in its wrong place may produce the most disastrous consequences. If we can weather the next fortnight without a convulsion, everything will then do. But just now the crisis is rather awful. There will, I have no doubt, be a great mob in Palace Yard to-day. It is quite wonderful, but I believe the people never had an idea that the Bill was in the slightest danger."

The debate was opened temperately enough by Ebrington's speech and Goulburn's reply to it, but in its progress took on inevitably a fiercer character. When the House had been ringing for hours with passionate cheers for the fiery harangues of Macaulay and Wetherall, and others as fiery though less eloquent than Macaulay's, then came at last the moment for Althorp to intervene. Never did his invaluable qualities as a man and a statesman find apter or more effective verbal expression than in the close of his speech on that critical night. He spoke thus :—

"I feel all the difficulties of my situation. I feel that this motion involves the conduct and character of the Government; and I therefore waited till the other members had delivered their opinions, wishing to learn the feelings and opinions of the House before I stated my own views, or before I undertook the defence of any of our measures. I have now heard the opinions of gentlemen, and will take the opportunity of saying a few words. From the opinions I have heard, it is stated that the conduct of the Government has not been such as to deserve the confidence of the House. The right honourable baronet (Sir Robert Peel) has adverted to the financial measures, and to the foreign policy, and to that still more important subject, the present state of the public feeling, for which he holds his Majesty's Government responsible. As to our financial measures, I will not now enter into any detail respecting them. Certainly, what I proposed on that subject did not meet with the approbation of the House; but I have the satisfaction, nevertheless, to know that several of my propositions were attended with beneficial consequences. It has been said that the remission of the tax on coals has not been productive of any good effect. In the immediate neighbourhood of town I allow that it has not, but in the remoter districts prices have fallen. Then, with respect to the remission of the tax on printed cottons. I have the satisfaction of knowing that in the manufacturing districts it has had a great and beneficial effect. So that, admitting that the larger portion of the measures which I proposed did not experience the concurrence of the House, yet others have given much relief. On our foreign policy I will also abstain from entering into details. But we have the satisfaction to say that we have preserved peace. One of the first pledges that we gave on entering upon office was, that we would endeavour to do so. We have redeemed that pledge, and there is no danger whatever that the present peace will be broken. As to the other most important point to which the right honourable baronet alluded, namely, the present state of public feeling, I maintain that for that state the present Government are not answerable. When we came into office, we found a strong and universal desire existing for Parliamentary Reform. That desire had been increasing for many years. The right honourable baronet and his friends were obliged to acknowledge its existence; and so strongly had it operated on the right honourable baronet's mind, that he allowed it had induced him on one occasion (before the introduction of the late Bill) to abstain from voting in that House on the question of Reform. Such was the state of feeling when he came into office, and when my noble friend at the head of the Administration gave that pledge on the subject of Reform which was consistent with all the principles of his public life. It has been insinuated by a right honourable and gallant officer that his Majesty's Government increased the extent of their measure of Reform because they found that they had lost the confidence of the late House of Commons. Now, I will ask, who that knew the composition and character of the late House of Commons would, in his senses, have proposed to them an extended measure of Reform in consequence of our having lost their confidence? Does the right honourable and gallant member recollect the sort of impression which the measure made on its introduction into the late House? An impression so strong, that I am convinced, if the House had divided on the first night, the Bill would have been thrown out by an immense majority. It was only after consideration, and after the sense of the country had declared itself in favour of the Bill, that we obtained the small majority that we did obtain. It was not we who excited the feeling in favour of Reform; but, that feeling existing, it would have been very dangerous to have brought in a delusive measure which would have disappointed the people. Undoubtedly, having passed the measure for the Reform of the Representation by a great majority in this House, and having sent it to the other House of Parliament, we did expect that at least it would have been taken into consideration. In that expectation we have been disappointed.

"The right honourable baronet says that this motion is unnecessary. I do not mean to say that my noble friend did not previously tell me of his intention to propose such a motion; but the step was taken entirely without our suggestion. The object of the motion—whether right or wrong, it is not for me to say—is, that if the House thinks that the removal of the present ministers from his Majesty's Councils would have a disastrous effect on public affairs, it was desirable that the House should express a strong confidence in those ministers. It may be necessary that I should speak frankly and freely on the subject. For myself, I declare that unless I felt a reasonable hope that a measure as efficient as that recently passed in this House might be secured by our continuance in office, I would not continue in office an hour. Whenever that hope ceases, I will cease to hold office. Both my colleagues and myself owe too much to our sovereign—we are too deeply indebted for the kindness, the candour, the frank sincerity which we have uniformly experienced from him—to desert the service of the king while his Majesty thinks our services valuable, and we ourselves think we can advantageously serve his Majesty. But we can no longer serve his Majesty advantageously if we sacrifice our character. Whatever may be the consequences of our retirement, it is our duty not to sacrifice our character. We owe also a great deal to the people. We have been supported by the people in the most handsome manner. The people have a right to demand that we should not desert them while our stay in office can conduce to their benefit. Sir, I will further state that I will not be a party to the proposal of any measure less efficient than that lately passed in this House. I do not mean to say that, after the discussion and consideration which the measure underwent, some modification may not be made in it, which, without diminishing its efficiency, may render it more complete. But what I mean to say is, that I will be no party to any measure which I do not conscientiously believe will give the people a full, free, and fair representation in Parliament, and secure all the objects which we hoped to effect for them by the late Bill. It is impossible that his Majesty's present Government can make any other proposition to the House. I admit that the opponents of the Bill have had a great triumph; although, in the present debate, with the exception of one honourable gentleman, no great triumph has been expressed. But I am confident that the measure is only postponed. I am satisfied that if the people of England will be firm and determined, but at the same time peaceable and quiet, there can be no doubt of their ultimate, and even speedy, success. There is one, and only one, chance of failure and disappointment; I mean any occurrence that may lead the people to break out into acts of violence, or into any unconstitutional conduct. If I have any influence with the people, if they put any trust in my sincerity—I implore them, for the sake of the great cause in which we are engaged, to be patient and peaceable, and to do nothing illegal or unconstitutional. I would say to them, Be as firm, be as determined, be as persevering, as you please; but never break through legal and constitutional restraints; never place yourselves in a situation in which the law must be put in operation against you, whoever are ministers. By temperance, steadiness, and perseverance, the cause of Parliamentary Reform must ultimately triumph. Whether my colleagues and myself are destined to have the honour of success upon that question as ministers, or whether, as in the Catholic question, after we have fought the battle, others are to enjoy the glory of victory, I know not; but as long as I have any voice in the direction of public affairs, I will use my utmost exertions in the cause of Parliamentary Reform."

These frank, simple, and resolute words did more to confirm and encourage his own followers, while at the same time calming and conciliating his opponents, than could have been done by any of the sublimest flights of elaborate or impassioned rhetoric. They were felt to be the expression of a magnanimous serenity, and of an unmistakable and unflinching resolve. The House divided, and the vote of confidence in the ministry was carried by a majority of 131. On the 20th of October Parliament was prorogued.

It was impossible, unfortunately, that Althorp's tranquillizing presence should be everywhere at once. Nor is it surprising that the "political unions" which had been formed throughout the country in support of Reform should have found his constancy easier to imitate than his calm. At a meeting of 150,000 men, the Birmingham Union, having voted thanks to Althorp and Russell for their services in Parliament, voted also that if the Lords were allowed to crush the Bill they would refuse to pay taxes. Althorp, in acknowledging the letter which told him of the vote of thanks, did not fail to express his censure of this threat. It began to seem as though the Government might have to combat the forces of disorder on one side as well as those of obstruction on the other. Among the crowds moved by genuine, if exaggerated, political excitement, there began to appear the usual admixture of rowdies and thieves. In Edinburgh, Derby, and Nottingham there had been riots involving serious damage to property and some loss of life. A rascally rabble had disgraced the streets of London by hooting the Duke of Wellington, and breaking the windows of Apsley House. At the end of October came the worst disturbance of all, the notorious Bristol riots, followed by the tragic suicide of Colonel Brereton, who was too sensitive to await the result of the court-martial which must have acquitted him of all dishonour. On the day when Bristol was in confusion, Althorp was on his way, after a scanty ten days' rest at Wiseton, to rejoin his colleagues in town at a Cabinet meeting. Besides their responsibilities for order, the ministry had to face the possibility of a reaction against Reform among the middle classes, who had hitherto given it good support, if they should find the cause associated with lawless force. With the king, too, there was the same danger to be feared. Owing partly to his anxious desire, a royal proclamation was issued on the 22nd of November, warning the people against the illegalities into which some of the political unions had lapsed.

Notwithstanding this proclamation, the Birmingham Union and their energetic chairman, Attwood, persevered in their intention to call a great meeting at the end of the month—a meeting which was formally to organize the non-payment of taxes; and at this meeting the members of the Union were called upon to appear in arms. It was a trying moment for the Government. Were they to suppress, in what might be a long and bloody conflict, a meeting of their own friends, aiming at lawful ends though by unlawful means? Or were they to connive at what might be the beginning of anarchy? In this dilemma Althorp came forward, and proved more emphatically than ever that if he commonly chose an unobtrusive part, it was not from any shrinking from responsibility in a time of need. He sent to the chairman of the Birmingham Union a private message by a friend and colleague of Attwood, urgently representing the evils of the proposed meeting, and the necessity that it should be given up. This private communication was made expressly and solely on Althorp's own behalf, without committing the Government to anything whatever in their collective capacity. It was, as Althorp afterwards said himself, "a very hazardous step," but it was justified both by its cause and by its effect. The leaders of the Union did what they probably would have done at no other man's request, and the armed meeting was countermanded.

Meanwhile the time was drawing near when the difficulties and dangers of the conflict of the two Houses must again be faced in Parliament, and some resource discovered for surmounting them. Some of the ministry were for putting off the session into the next year, but Althorp was strong against delay, and after a division of the Cabinet his view prevailed. Parliament was summoned to meet on the 6th of December, and on the 12th Russell moved for leave to bring in a third Reform Bill. It differed little from the last, such differences as there were being mostly in consequence of the completion of the new census. Nor was its reception by the Tory leaders changed. Conscious of some wavering in the ranks behind him, Peel hastened to announce his unaltered antagonism; and by a somewhat ungenerous attack on the motives of the ministry, drew forth a spirited reply from Althorp, which seems to have left the honours of that first night with him, and to have at once conciliated opponents and encouraged his own side. The Bill was read a first time without a division, and on the second reading only two nights were occupied by debate. It gave opportunity for the brilliant speeches of Macaulay and Stanley; that of the latter being a reply to Croker, and a cogent exposition of the historical facts derived by Stanley from the greater learning of Hobhouse. Peel exerted all his eloquence to rally his party; but though none of them would vote for the Bill, some declined to vote against it. When the division came, early in the morning of Sunday, the 18th, the Bill passed by a majority of 162 in a House of 486.

After a Christmas recess of a month the House met again on the 17th of January. The Scotch and Irish Reform Bills were brought in and read the first time, and on the 20th the House went into committee on the English Bill. The sittings of the committee were protracted to the middle of March. Every night of these laborious sittings Althorp was in his place, and had to conduct long and arduous arguments on technical points against such potent legal antagonists as Scarlett, Wetherall, Sugden, Pollock, ranged formidably on the benches of the Opposition. By virtue of a clear head and, still more, of his absolute and absorbing identification, so to speak, with the Bill, every clause of which he knew perfectly in all its bearings, he held his own. In a private memorandum, written after his death, Brougham says of him, " His ability was never so remarkably shown as on the Reform Bill, both years, 1831 and 1832. He had a knowledge of its whole details, and of all the numberless matters connected with it, which was almost supernatural. The others knew it so ill, and got into such scrapes when opposed to the most formidable opposition of Croker chiefly (who had something like Althorp's mastery of the subject), that it became quite necessary to prevent them from speaking—or what was then called 'to put on the muzzle'—and Althorp really did the whole. Then his temper was of course admirable, and quite invariably equal. Sugden said he had learnt a lesson from Althorp—or, at least, that it was his own fault if he had not—which was not ill said." Macaulay had already remarked, in a letter written near the end of the preceding session, "Althorp has done more service even as a debater than all the other ministers together, Stanley excepted."

At last the committee reported, the report was considered, and on the 19th of March the third reading was moved. After three more nights of debate the Bill passed by a majority of 116 in a House of 594.

All the labour and anxiety of the winter had only brought things again to the point where they had stood at the end of last September, six months before. The stone had been painfully rolled up the hill again; was it to roll back once more, or to be triumphantly borne over the brow, to become the corner-stone of an enduring fabric? Once more Althorp and Russell, at the head of their party in the Commons, appeared in the House of Lords, carrying with them the Bill, and "requesting the concurrence of their lordships to the same." It was felt throughout the country that that request must now be made for the last time. As the phrase then went, men were asking now not merely, What will the Lords do? but also, What must be done with the Lords? Could they be persuaded, or must they be coerced? All the wishes of the ministry were sincerely and strenuously bent on persuasion. The utmost care was taken by them to avoid all appearance of dictation or a peremptory attitude, to welcome all overtures and approaches, to build a golden bridge for "their friend the enemy" in retreat. So great was Grey's anxiety for the success of the Bill in the Lords, and so great his admiration of Althorp's conduct of it through the Commons, that he even pressed him to take a peerage, in order that he might be present in person to take charge of the measure in the Upper House. It was, of course an impracticable proposal, and was soon recognized as such by Grey, for Althorp could not be spared from the leadership of the Commons; but the incident is of a significance worth recording. The Bill was read a first time in the Lords without debate, but with the encouraging circumstance that Wharncliffe and Harrowby, who had before opposed it, now promised to vote for the second reading. This was fixed for the 9th of April, and the debate then lasted four nights. It was begun and ended by Grey, with speeches of so admirable a tact and dignity as showed that thus far at least he was in no need of the aid which his modesty had asked from Althorp in that House. But the old counter-arguments were urged by the old voices, and very few waverers gave open adhesion to the repentance of Wharncliffe and Harrowby. The daylight had long dawned on the exhausted House when, about seven o'clock on the morning of the 14th of April, the division was taken. The Bill passed the second reading by a majority of 9 in a House of 359. It was saved so far, but it entered committee in circumstances ominously resembling those of the first Bill in the lately dissolved House of Commons, about the same time in the year before. The omen was disastrously fulfilled. After the Easter recess of three weeks the reactionaries rallied; and in committee, on the 7th of May, Lyndhurst's hostile amendment, postponing the disfranchisement clauses, was carried by a majority of 35 in a House of 267.

During the debate on this amendment Grey had held frequent and earnest consultation with Althorp below the bar of the House. When the hostile majority was announced, the Prime Minister promptly and boldly declared that he held the adoption of that amendment as equivalent to the rejection of the Bill.

There were two alternatives before the ministry—to create enough peers to swamp the hostile majority, or to resign. Althorp had for some time been far less reluctant than Grey to create peers.

He had not the same tenderness for the dignity of the House of Lords, where he was convinced that it was inflicting injury on the commonwealth. He believed, indeed, in the necessity of a second chamber, and consequently of not lightly over-riding it; but he was under no illusion as to his "order," nor disposed to think the opinion of the House of Lords, overweighted by the hereditary majority, of more intrinsic value than that of any other collection of three or four hundred men of the wealthier classes, at any rate on matters where their private interests were involved. At least two months before this date he had made up his mind for the creation of peers, and on the 10th of March had written to Grey a masterly and conclusive letter urging this view. Now at last Grey and the whole Cabinet were convinced of the necessity, and with one accord they requested the king to empower them formally for the act. But here occurred a not wholly unexpected obstacle. The king, who had persuaded himself that things would after all go smoothly, could not muster resolution for so bold a step. He shrank from giving decisive consent, and the ministry had no choice but to resign.

Of Althorp's demeanour at this crisis we have

noteworthy evidence in a letter from Jeffrey to a friend. He thus describes his morning interview: "I had a characteristic scene with that most frank, true, and stout-hearted of God's creatures, Lord Althorp. I was led up to his dressing-room, where I found him in a dressing-gown, his arms bare, his beard half-shaved, with a desperate razor in one hand, and a great soap-brush in the other. He gave me the loose finger of his brush-hand, and with the usual twinkle of his bright eye and a radiant smile, he said, 'You need not be anxious about your Scotch Bills to-night, as I have the pleasure to tell you we are no longer his Majesty's ministers.'"

Althorp, in fact, with his customary political instinct, saw what many others were just then not cool enough to see, that the present check, alarming as it seemed, was to be of very short duration, and that the triumph of Reform was now virtually assured. At the same time we may consider that, notwithstanding this assurance, he concealed no slight anxiety beneath his light-hearted demeanour. Those who knew him intimately bear witness to his self-control in encouraging others by his cheerfulness and ease when he was weary and heart-sick himself. His fear at present was not that Reform would be ultimately rejected, but that in the intervals deeds of violence might be done. On the whole, the order and good sense of the political unions had been no less admirable than their earnestness; and they were free from all blame for the riots which had occurred here and there in the winter before. But the events of the last week were producing a feeling of exasperation in men who were incapable of riot, but might be capable of civil war. At many places, when the news came of the resignation of the ministry, the bells of churches and chapels were tolled all night. It was officially reported from Birmingham and from Buckinghamshire that if there should be a rising in this cause, no respectable man would act as a special constable to put it down. A manufacturer had offered to supply the Birmingham Union with ten thousand muskets at fifteen shillings apiece. Others, who would have opposed all violence or use of arms, were beginning to advise a passive resistance to law by a refusal to pay taxes until the Bill was passed. This was actually done by Lord Milton, though the prompt and happy issue of affairs deprived his act of consequence. And not only in the excitement of the moment, but also long afterwards, in the calm review of history, a good deal has been written to maintain that this attitude toward the law, at least in the second and milder form, was not only excusable but justifiable. This certainly is a question worth asking—If the resistance of the House of Lords had continued, would a loyal citizen have been justified in answering it by a disobedience to the law, which is above Commons, Lords, and King alike? The answer must, I think, be in the negative, however keen our sympathies with the cause of the Reformers. If men find any law or ordinance under which they live so intolerably bad as to suggest illegal resistance to it, the first thing they have to ask themselves is whether there is adequate cause for civil war. If not, then sporadic acts of resistance, such as obstruction of the officers of the law enforcing authority, are disastrous folly, and the incitement thereto is cruel and dastardly crime. If, on the other hand, they deliberately elect the terrible alternative of civil war, they may be only following the example of some of the most loyal patriots and truest benefactors of mankind. The English should be the last people to forget this. But in the present case there was by no means a complete analogy with the situation in England in 1641 or in 1688. It was not for refusing to change the constitution, but for unlawful usurpation of privilege, that the Stuart kings were met by resistance in arms. The case of Hampden afforded no precedent justifying the Reformers in refusing to pay taxes, for Hampden refused on the ground of the illegality of the tax. The Long Parliament and their adherents took up arms, partly to resist what they honestly believed to be arbitrary innovations in Church and State, partly to enforce legal obligations of compact evaded by Charles I. It was that evasion which caused, and probably justified, the counter-aggression of the Parliament in demanding control of the militia. But in the crisis of 1832 there was no doubt that the House of Lords was in its legal right in rejecting the Bill, and the king in his legal right in refusing to create peers—at any rate while it seemed possible that another ministry could be formed which would advise him differently. The Manchester Union recognized the true constitutional *ultimatum* in sending a petition to the House of Commons, praying the House to grant no supplies until the Bill was passed unimpaired. This petition was followed within a few days by many others with the same prayer. Of course, if the minority of the nation had, after full trial of alternative ministries, refused to support the only one which could obtain supplies, and had thus chosen to reduce the country to anarchy, then the will of the majority must ultimately have been carried into effect by force. But the situation was still very far from having reached any such appalling deadlock as this. To the calm judgment of later generations, it is plain that it was a mere matter of waiting a few days or weeks for the position of forces to unfold itself unmistakably. But at the moment, after more than a year of the strain of eager hopes and bitter disappointments, of the most intense political excitement that had possessed the country since the Revolution of 1688, it was impossible to be wholly dispassionate, however loyally passion might be controlled. It is to the enduring honour of the imperial English race that, with rare exceptions, they showed in this great crisis that they could govern themselves as well as others, nobly and faithfully maintaining the watchwords of the Unions, "Peace, Order, Obedience to the Law."

The resolve of the Reformers in Parliament was not less firm than in the country. When, on the evening of the 8th of May, Althorp entered the

House of Commons, he was, in the words of the *Times* of the next day, "instantly hailed with enthusiastic cheers and cries, accompanied by plaudits both of hands and feet." When the cheers at last were over, he rose, and announced the resignation of the ministry. The feeling of the House expressed itself, first by more cheering, then by a notice from Ebrington, agreed on by the Liberals the day before, that on the morrow he would move an address to the Crown on the present state of public affairs. The only protest against this step came, characteristically enough, from Althorp himself, who was chivalrously reluctant to embarrass in any way the king or his prospective ministry before knowing what solution they would suggest. The next day, after spending some hours in buying flowers for his father's garden at Althorp, and writing out directions for their planting, he went to attend the debate on Ebrington's motion. In the course of this debate he was called on by Baring to explain the grounds of the resignation of the ministry. As the resignation had that morning been formally accepted by the king, Althorp was now free to explain the cause. He answered thus: "The advice we thought it our duty to offer to his Majesty was that he should create a number of peers sufficient to enable us to carry the Reform Bill in an efficient form." These words were greeted by a tumult of acclamation, not less loud and long than that which had welcomed him the day before. After a debate, of which the chief feature was a spirit-stirring speech from Macaulay, the division was taken on Ebrington's motion. It was carried by a majority of 80 in a comparatively small House of 496.

Meanwhile Wellington and Lyndhurst were trying to form an administration. In the course of two or three days the duke learnt far more of the true nature of the situation than he had known or realized since the conflict of powers began. Peel, who seems to have been less than his best self on this occasion, hung back in helpless perplexity both from taking office and from the frank admission of defeat which was the only alternative. Wellington had to act without him, and acted as his principles required. He had been anxious that a great political experiment which he thought rash should not be tried, but he was infinitely more anxious that nothing should prevent, in his famous phrase, the king's government from being carried on. Whatever enthusiastic civilians might think, the duke, who had seen something of civil war, was very certain that this matter was not worth it. On the 9th of May the Liberal ministers had resigned; on the 15th, by the duke's advice, the repentant king requested them to take office again; and on the 17th he had promised that it should be on their own terms. The Lords were to be constrained into acquiescence, but before resorting to the extreme measure of swamping their House by new creations, an opportunity of surrender was to be given to it by the celebrated circular letter written by Sir Herbert Taylor, the king's private secretary, on the king's behalf—a step said to have been suggested by Sir Herbert himself. It ran thus :—

"MY DEAR LORD,
"I am honoured with his Majesty's commands to acquaint your lordship that all difficulties as to the arrangements in progress will be obviated by a declaration in the House to-night, from a sufficient number of peers, that in consequence of the present state of affairs they have come to the resolution of dropping their further opposition to the Reform Bill; so that it may pass without delay, and as nearly as possible in its present shape."

That evening the Commons had assembled in an excited and dangerous mood. The recalled ministers, during their final negotiation with the king, had observed a scrupulous reticence, and abstained from giving their supporters any positive assurance of success. Under the strain of this final suspense, the Reformers began to grow resentfully suspicious of some possible frustration of their hope, by which after all they might find themselves baffled and betrayed. But when the House had filled, Althorp rose amid a sudden and anxious silence. In a cheerful voice, and with the serenity of a generous triumph in his face, he announced that he now had confident hope that he and his colleagues would remain in office, and that the Reform Bill would be passed. He gave no explanations, and was pressed for none by his followers. They knew their man, and what his words and tones were worth. There was an instant calm in their minds, for the leader they trusted had bidden them to be of good cheer.

The thing to be done was now done quickly. Within the next twenty-four hours all that had passed was everywhere known. The circular letter had its due effect on the peers. On receiving it, the greater part of the former non-contents absented themselves, and continued to do so while the Reform Bill passed rapidly through the House of Lords. On the 4th of June, 1832, the Bill was read the third time in that House, and on the 7th it received the royal assent, and became law.

CHAPTER VII.

FIRST YEAR OF THE REFORMED PARLIAMENT.

THE provisions of the English Reform Act as finally passed did not greatly differ from those of the original Bill introduced on the 1st of March, 1831 ; and the Scotch and Irish Acts, passed in the next month of the session, were generally on the same lines. All boroughs with a population of less than two thousand were disfranchised ; and under this head came fifty-six English boroughs which had hitherto returned one hundred and eleven members to Parliament. Those boroughs with less than four thousand inhabitants which had hitherto returned two members were henceforth to return but one; this enactment extinguished thirty-two more seats. Of the hundred and forty-three seats thus made assignable, eighty-four were given to new and large constituencies. The larger counties were divided, and sixty-five additional seats were assigned to them. The ten divisions of London and twelve other boroughs which had hitherto returned one member were now to return two, thus accounting for twenty-two more seats. The rest were given to large towns. Manchester, Leeds, Birmingham, and thirty-nine others were enfranchised, some receiving more than one seat. In Scotland the changes made were chiefly in the matter of boundaries, but here also the number of seats assigned to important towns was increased from fifteen to twenty-three. In Ireland there was the smaller increase from thirty-five to thirty-nine, and a second member was given to the University of Dublin.

In the matter of the qualification of voters, the franchise in boroughs was now founded on inhabitancy. The electors were to be the occupiers of dwellings of a yearly value of ten pounds. Borough corporations were deprived henceforth of the power of conferring the franchise, but the existing "freemen," if resident, were allowed to retain their privilege, those only excepted who had received it since the beginning of March, 1831, after which time the power of many town councils had been grossly abused to create voters who would oppose the Reform Bill. This change was of especial importance in Scotland and Ireland.

The county franchise, which had been confined to freeholders, was extended to leaseholders and copyholders, and, by the well-known "Chandos" clause, to tenants-at-will occupying at a yearly value of £50. The extension of the county franchise was much greater in England and Scotland than in Ireland, where a new settlement, disfranchising the forty-shilling freeholders and introducing the ten-pound limit, had already been made in 1829. It was calculated that in Great Britain the numbers of the electorate would be raised from some 200,000 to about 350,000.

This great change in the representative system made a new general election necessary; and when Parliament rose on the 14th of August, it was on the understanding that there would be a dissolution before the end of that year. Although the great struggle was over in June, the remaining two months of the session were by no means without labour and anxiety for Althorp and his colleagues. The passing of a Bill for the compulsory composition of Irish Tithe, and the opposition to the payment of a Russian-Dutch loan,* to which the ministry

---

* This was a loan made to Russia by a Dutch firm during the great French war. England had undertaken half the charge of the debt, on condition that the King of the Netherlands (who undertook the other half) remained sovereign in the Belgian provinces. These

tenaciously, and it would seem justly, held themselves to be bound, were both matters requiring delicate and firm handling, on which it was impossible to maintain the majorities of the divisions on Reform. The Budget, in view of the absorption of the session by other matters, could not be expected to do much more than continue the financial arrangements of the year before, and it received little opposition or criticism from the exhausted House. Then at last Althorp obtained, in September, three welcome weeks of greatly needed repose at Wiseton among his flocks and herds. Friends who had not seen him lately were startled by his altered looks, the sign of a strain on his constitution from which it never altogether recovered. For nearly two years he had now been undergoing the continuous pressure of laborious thought and speech, attended by harassing anxiety, on contingencies and responsibilities as grave and critical as ever engaged a statesman in time of peace.

This too short holiday was ended by the first meeting of the Cabinet on the 1st of October. Even

---

were now being made a separate State, but with unforeseen circumstances, and with the support of the British Government, which thus continued to be morally responsible for the charge.

then it seemed to Althorp that he and his colleagues had been too long absent from their posts. The arrears of attention due to other matters postponed during the long struggle over Reform now began to make themselves insistently felt. These matters, and the measures by which the ministry dealt with them, with Althorp's individual share in those measures, will be best touched on when they have been brought before the new Parliament.

The dissolution took place in December, and the new constituencies supported their creators. The Liberal successes in the boroughs much more than counterbalanced those cases in which the Tories regained their advantage in the counties. In Northamptonshire, after some uncertainty, it was finally arranged that the representation should be amicably divided, and that Althorp and a Tory colleague, Sir Charles Knightley, should be returned without a contest. On the 29th of January, 1833, the House met, and Althorp, by supporting the re-election of the Tory Speaker, Manners-Sutton, gave timely proof that the ministry were not disposed to make a tyrannous use of their majority. It was needed for more substantial and valuable ends.

During eight years from this time the Liberals

maintained an all but unbroken tenure of power; and whatever may have been the failures and disappointments of that period, especially of its latter part, it was undeniably a period in which great and memorable services were rendered to the honour and welfare of the country. For two years only of these eight was Althorp to remain in office and leader of the House of Commons. But those first two years were to be signalized by the two most illustrious achievements of the whole term—the abolition of colonial slavery, and the reform of the poor-law. It is the second and more arduous of these achievements which is peculiarly associated with Althorp's name.

There were many other fields of reform in which it was found impossible to clear the way by strokes of policy so trenchant and decisive as these. Of such fields, that which engaged the earliest and the most recurrent attention of the Parliament of 1833 was the condition of Ireland and of the Irish Church and Tithe. The Catholic Emancipation Act of 1829 had not by itself made the Irish Roman Catholics content. The existence of the Protestant Established Church was still a grievance, and one which many attendant circumstances united to emphasize and enhance. This Church, with less than one million members, was supported chiefly by tithes and Church-rates collected from more than six million Roman Catholics, who at the same time had to maintain their own clergy by offerings no less rigorously exacted, whether by compunction or commination, than was the tax imposed by law. The minute division of the land made the collection of the tithe additionally obtrusive and vexatious. In seasons of distress the feeling of grievance among the peasantry grew into the fiercest exasperation. Collectors of tithe and Church-rate were now habitually attacked and not seldom murdered. The clergy of the Establishment were starving on their invidious legal rights. Their own Archbishop of Dublin declared that "the continuance of the tithe system could only be through a kind of civil war." Such an institution called aloud for legislation, as also did the disorder into which it had helped to plunge a large part of the island.

Irish difficulties were further complicated and aggravated by the personal characteristics of those men who at this time were most concerned with them. When the Grey ministry came in, in 1830, the Irish appointments seem to have been left at the disposal of Lord Anglesey, the reinstated Lord-Lieutenant. Though tolerant and liberal himself, and endeared to the Irish Catholics by his former administration, he allotted these places to men in whom personal knowledge led him to confide, without regard to the fact that they, unlike himself, had been opponents of the Emancipation Act, and must therefore be unpopular; and without regarding the plausibility of the claims of O'Connell and his supporters, who had expected that the removal of religious disabilities would involve a practical recognition of their own eligibility to appointments in the Irish administration. Nor was the choice of Stanley for Irish Secretary destined to prove felicitous. In the career of Stanley, afterwards to be a Tory Prime Minister, we may see an illustration of the tendency toward that preponderant influence of rhetorical facility which has had graver effects in later and more important instances. He was an admirable debater, of great use in the Reform struggle, and at all times capable of making a most effective speech from instructions supplied to him. But neither in temper, knowledge, tact, ideas, or administrative capacity was he fitted for the post of Irish Secretary. It soon appeared that some of his strongest convictions, to which he honestly adhered in opposition to his colleagues, were such as had a special and disastrous effect on his view of the most pressing of Irish concerns; and these convictions ultimately led to his resignation. Not till Melbourne's premiership did the Liberal Government succeed in finding the most suitable men to appoint to office in Ireland. This was, indeed, the one feature of importance in which the latter part of the decade of Liberal Government does not compare unfavourably with the earlier part.

But the most important personal influence in Ireland at this time was that of O'Connell. A copious and impassioned oratory, and an extraordinary talent for energetic organization, were the means by which he made and maintained his power. But the wide extent of that power was due to his having obtained, in the view of the Irish Roman Catholics, the position of their recognized champion against the oppression of Orange Ascendency—that Ascendency which the rapid changes of the last twenty years have made it difficult for us to realize as it once was. The men who till then had affected to represent Ireland, and abused their usurped power to prey on her, belonged mainly to the landlord class; not, as now, to the classes of publicans, newspaper-writers, lawyers, and money-lenders. In occupying this championship of the Catholics, O'Connell had lately survived a succession of discreditable incidents, which might well have ruined him in the eyes, not only of his opponents, but also of his adherents. There was, indeed, nothing to discredit him in the fact of the subscription of the "rent" or "tribute" of some ten thousand a year on which he lived, for he had given up a lucrative practice at the Bar for politics; though in the manner of collecting the money there was much that was needlessly unseemly. But he had shown at times a signal absence of trustworthiness and of self-respect. He had defaced his triumph in the matter of the Clare election by his reckless words and acts; not, indeed, unprovoked, but much in excess of the provocation. He had loudly proclaimed that nothing should make him abandon the forty-shilling freeholders, and then had passively acquiesced in their disfranchisement. In October, 1830, he insulted the then Irish Secretary, Sir Henry Hardinge; and when called to account for his language, O'Connell first shuffled about the expressions he had used, and then declined to fight. This conduct he repeated on other occasions, and it was not the less damaging that he sometimes allowed his sons to accept the challenges sent to him. He marred the effect of his great eloquence by grotesque and monotonous invective. All action which offended him was indiscriminately "base, bloody, and brutal." Descending to the level of the worse sort of the politicians of his island, he seemed often to have lost the self-control proper to the savage without acquiring that proper to the civilized man. Althorp himself, the most tolerant of men, says in a letter to Sir Herbert Taylor, written in February, 1833, when O'Connell was acting inimically to the Liberal Government : "So far O'Connell has played our game ; he has disgusted the House by the delay, and still more by the extreme vulgarity and coarseness of his manners. He appears to be almost insane. Before this session, however violent his language, he was always gentlemanlike in his manners ; but all appearance of this is now thrown aside." Two months before, Russell wrote to Moore : "When I want to say anything in favour of Liberal measures to the Irish, O'Connell's conduct takes the argument out of my mouth." Even regarding merely his Irish constituents, this misconduct of O'Connell was a gross injury to them, for it inevitably deprived him of respect and attention when he urged their grievances. Nevertheless they long continued to repose an almost boundless confidence in him, simply as the most eloquent exponent of the wrongs done by Protestant and landlord Ascendency; and if he could do nothing in guiding, he could at least do much in disturbing, the political history of these times, and the success of the Liberal administration. Of definite and continuous policy he seems to have had but little. It was perhaps impossible for him to do much to reconcile the conflicting elements in Ireland; at any rate, he only followed the example of Orange intolerance in exasperating those elements against each other. His sovereign prescription for the discords of his island was the Repeal of that Union with Great Britain which offered the only prospect of ultimately merging local animosities by real incorporation in a greater whole.

Within the last few years the question of Repeal of the Union has, through a singular coincidence of conditions, suddenly attained prominence and excited absorbing interest; so that the arguments on both sides are now too familiar to need mention. It will be enough to recall one or two facts which placed the question on a somewhat different footing when Grey and Althorp were in office. Not a single public man of repute in any party, or who had borne the responsibility of office, looked upon Repeal as deserving serious consideration. On the other hand, there are at least two important arguments used against it now which could not have been used then. The first is the impracticability and danger of allowing the existence of an independent executive, responsible only to the proposed Irish Parliament. This was not demanded by O'Connell, nor had it existed before the Union. The second argument is the fact that the people of Great Britain have now proved themselves so sincerely bent on removing Irish grievances that these may safely be referred to the Imperial Parliament. In 1833 this could not have been so confidently said. The inhabitants of over-crowded Ireland were indeed at that time a much more important fraction of the population of the United Kingdom than at present, being then nearly a third of the whole, instead of about an eighth, as they now are. Yet there was not only great apathy and ignorance in England and Scotland as to Irish concerns; there was also a widespread sentiment of Protestant intolerance, and excessive jealousy of concessions to a Church which was still looked upon by many as making claims on its members incompatible with their loyalty to the commonwealth. George the Third and George the Fourth, in their opposition to the removal of religious disabilities, only represented the prejudice of what was probably the majority of their subjects; though the prejudice was not vehement enough in most of them to resist the better judgment of Parliament in the emancipation of 1829. The almost total disappearance of this religious intolerance toward Irish Catholicism in Great Britain is now one of the brightest and most encouraging circumstances to be taken into account in dealing with Irish problems. But at that time it existed in strength enough to be a serious embarrassment to a Liberal ministry. Any such sweeping measure as the Disestablishment of the Irish Church it would have been hopeless for them to propose. They had to work toward their end by incomplete measures, which were all that could be attempted with any chance of success, until fuller knowledge and sympathy could grow up between the islands. But Althorp and his Liberal colleagues were as steadfastly convinced as any Unionist of to-day that a Repeal of the Union could only mean the substitution of one Ascendency for another, and must, therefore, be as incompatible with the principles of their party as with the honour and welfare of the whole Commonwealth of the British Isles.

Two Bills were prepared by the Irish Secretary and submitted to the Cabinet—one dealing with Church temporalities, the other with the suppression of disturbances. With neither of these was Althorp satisfied. The former seemed to him timid and narrow in its scope, the latter over-stringent in its provisions. So strong was his dissatisfaction, that he placed his resignation in the Prime Minister's hands. The reply was a letter from Grey, expressing profound distress and depression at the prospect. "The consequence," he said, of Althorp's resignation, "would be to destroy the Whig party for ever; to give power in the first instance to those whose principles we have always opposed, and eventually perhaps, for such a Government could not last, to produce a subversion of the Government itself. With such a prospect before me, I will bear much, I will suffer much, whilst a choice is left me. But that choice I shall no longer have, if you resign." After this appeal, and further entreaties when he met his chief,

Althorp consented to remain, on condition that both Bills should undergo modifications which would make it possible for him to support them. These were not obtained without some further resistance from Stanley; and the embarassments caused by the Irish Secretary were not confined to his action in the Cabinet. Before Parliament met he had made an election speech in Lancashire, in which he had used such expressions about the Irish agitators as were construed by them into a threat of their forcible suppression. So much was his popularity impaired, even among English and Scotch Liberals, that the Cabinet fell back once more on Althorp's authority with the House, and entrusted to him, instead of to Stanley, the introduction of the Irish measures. On February 12, he explained that which dealt with the Irish Church. Its main provisions were the abolition of Church-rates in Ireland, and the reduction of the number of bishops from twenty-two to twelve. This reduction was estimated to effect a saving of something over £60,000 a year—a sum nearly equal to that which the Church would lose by the abolition of the rate, or "cess." The place of the Church-rate, however, was to be supplied by a graduated tax on Church property (excluding benefices of less than £200 a year). This tax was to be paid to commissioners, who were to spend it on the repair of churches and other ecclesiastical purposes. The money saved by the extinction of bishoprics might be dealt with at the pleasure of Parliament.

Althorp's exposition of this measure, which he had done his utmost to broaden, and his cordially sympathetic tone toward Irish grievances, procured a favourable reception for the Bill on all hands. O'Connell cheered loudly, and for some days was warm in praising the Government which he had covered with abuse in the debate on the address.

The Disturbances Bill was introduced three days later in the Lords by Grey, and passed on the 22nd of February. It enacted not only that the Lord-Lieutenant might suppress meetings and declare districts to be in a state of disturbance, but also in such districts offenders were to be tried by courts-martial. The Bill was to be brought in on the 27th in the House of Commons. This duty also was imposed on Althorp, and was much less efficiently performed by him. His hesitation as to the expediency of some of the provisions, especially as to the courts-martial, showed too transparently through his speech. The Cabinet would, after all, have been wiser to have left the exposition of the Bill to its real author, Stanley. Had not he intervened with an eloquent and cogent speech in its support, the Bill might have been rejected. As it was, however, its passing was assured by what Russell afterwards called "one of the greatest triumphs ever won in a popular assembly by the power of oratory." The Bill passed with only slight alterations, and involved a fresh alienation of O'Connell and his group— unmindful, perhaps, of the more stringent "coercion acts" constantly in force under the Irish Parliament which they wished to revive. This alienation was not diminished by the fate of the Church Bill. It was handled in an unfriendly spirit by the Lords, and, to conciliate them, the "appropriation clause," which provided that the revenues of the superfluous bishoprics should be freely disposed of by Parliament, was abandoned. It was Stanley himself who moved the omission of the clause, which he had been only induced to accept in the Cabinet by the pressure of Althorp and the more thorough reformers. With this serious mutilation, and a few smaller amendments, the Bill passed the Lords on the 30th of July. But much earlier in the session it had been already felt by Stanley as well as by his colleagues that though he had achieved something of a personal triumph, it was inexpedient that he should remain at the Irish Office. Durham's retirement toward the end of March made a reconstruction of the ministry possible. Hobhouse became Irish Secretary, and Goderich Privy Seal; while Stanley succeeded Goderich at the Colonial Office.

It was from that office that the most memorable and beneficent measure of the year 1833 proceeded—the abolition of colonial slavery, at the national cost of twenty million pounds. But neither Stanley nor Althorp, nor any one minister or any one party, is to be credited with any peculiar share in this great act of justice and mercy, whereby three-quarters of a million of slaves were freed. Its real achievers were the men holding no political office, who had sworn the destruction of slavery beneath the British flag, and had undergone years of toilsome drudgery, of cost and privation, of misrepresentation and of disappointment, in labouring to achieve that end. Of these, the most eminent survivors were the aged Clarkson and Zachary Macaulay; and their most devoted coadjutor in Parliament was Sir Thomas Fowell Buxton. Wilberforce too lived just long enough to see this consummation of his desire. The labour of preparing the Bill fell most heavily on the chief permanent officials, especially James Stephen, counsel to the Colonial Department—a labour scantily acknowledged by Stanley. It can hardly be doubted that slavery must have been abolished about this time by public opinion, whatever ministry had been in power. The chief merit which could be shown in the matter by a Chancellor of the Exchequer was the willingness to face such discontent as might be caused by the taxation needed to supply the twenty millions, after the popular enthusiasm had subsided, and the reason for the demand on their purses had faded from the minds of men. In the words (perhaps over-strong) of Lord Russell forty years afterwards, "it was one thing to estimate the loss which the planters would incur; it was another to obtain from Parliament means to defray the charge. This could only be done by Lord Althorp, the responsible minister for the National Exchequer. Lord Althorp did not shrink from this appalling task." The Act of Abolition was passed in August, 1833, and slavery in the British Empire was to cease in August, 1834.

A kindred measure, and under kindred conditions, was passed in the same month on behalf of an oppressed class nearer home. By a Bill introduced by Lord Ashley, and afterwards committed to Althorp's charge, the labour of children in factories under thirteen years of age was limited to eight hours a day; and no boy or girl under eighteen was to be employed more than sixty-nine hours in the week. This Act was happily only the first of many important and anxiously considered measures by which the evils of industrial competition have been gradually mitigated; and grievous as these evils still are in some industries they are at least less grievous in England than in any other manufacturing country in Europe. For this auspicious measure also no one party or minister can claim credit; the real credit is due to unofficial men. But the fact that the Reformed Parliament in its first session had abolished slavery, reduced the abuses of the Irish Church, and diminished the hardships of the children of the poor,—this could not but be a source of pride and encouragement to the ministry which had identified itself with Reform.

And though these had so far been the greatest, they were by no means the only achievements of the new administration. Monopoly and privilege were in many new quarters unsparingly subordinated to the common weal. In the course of this session landed property was at last made subject to simple contract debts. It was now fourteen years since Althorp had unsuccessfully struggled to carry this provision in the Insolvent Debtors Bill which he introduced in 1819. In the preceding session he had destroyed another invidious privilege of his class in circumstances which give good proof of his peculiar earnestness in reforms of this kind. Landowners have always been especially tenacious of the exclusive rights given them by game laws. Under a statute of Charles II.'s time, only landowners and their heirs were entitled to kill game; and could only licence another to do so by a "deputation" fictitiously appointing him gamekeeper. The sale of game was also absolutely prohibited. These restrictions had been maintained against the occasional attacks of reformers until the return of a Liberal majority in 1831. Then Althorp, with all the weight of the Reform Bill on his shoulders, brought in and passed a Game Act which, by the testimony of contemporaries, cost him great trouble and patience to carry through Parliament. It abolished the old feudal restrictions, and enacted that it should be lawful for any one to shoot or sell game on obtaining a licence from the Inland Revenue Office. The time chosen by Althorp for this task, though very burdensome for himself, was opportune for the Bill. The majority of the House of Lords, who at another time would probably have thrown it out, were just then so much absorbed in opposing Parliamentary Reform, and so loth to lose popularity on any minor issue, that they suffered this invasion of their cherished privileges to pass.

This is but one instance of the increasing pressure which was gradually bearing down the barriers of monopolies of all kinds. Religious equality had already won its most signal triumphs in the Acts of 1828 and 1829, removing the chief disabilities of Protestant and Roman Catholic Nonconformists; and the stream continued to flow in the same direction. Commercial monopolies were being gradually invaded by a series of smaller changes leading up to the larger triumphs of Free Trade, which were now not far off. Parliament itself was now surrendering the more indefensible privileges of its members. Their exemption from arrest for debt had virtually lost its importance when the Reform Act put an end to the sale of borough seats. Their exemption from the penalties of those ecclesiastical courts which still retained jurisdiction in cases of probate was now abolished in 1833, by a Bill introduced in the House of Lords by Brougham.

The Lord Chancellor's reforms in legal procedure, especially in Chancery, belong to a field to which only brief reference can be made here. But they are partly attributable to the same impulse against monopolies, as the obstructions which had hitherto prevented them consisted not seldom in privileges attached to some place-holding class or individual. They were considerable in themselves, and attracted additional attention by the eloquence with which Brougham urged them in Parliament, and the vivacity he infused into his subject. The general feeling was expressed by a county member, who, after listening to the Chancellor's great speech on Chancery reform at the beginning of the session of 1831, said admiringly, "This is prodigiously fine indeed. Why, Brougham puts one in mind of Demosthenes, or some of those fellows one reads of at school."

At the Foreign Office also the country's work was being well done by Palmerston. Friendly and even cordial relations were established with the new constitutional monarchy in France, notwithstanding the hazardous points sometimes raised in the settlement of the new state of Belgium; notwithstanding also King William's dislike of a French alliance. On one occasion, at least, he expressed this with astounding recklessness,* and there was, of course, abundance of national prejudice to echo his rash words. But there were no issues abroad at that time which seemed to touch England nearly; and if Palmerston's skilful firmness in negotiation could not do much to increase the reputation of ministers among the people at large, they at any rate suffered no loss of credit on this side of their administration.

Yet, notwithstanding all the good work which was being accomplished since the passing of the Reform Act, and was to be maintained with no less vigour during the remaining year of Althorp's tenure of office, contemporary records agree in affirming that the popularity of the ministry in the country had already begun slowly to decline. Perhaps this was no more than was to be expected, as a certain consequence of the nature of nations and of man. During the long and exciting struggle

---

* In a speech to a regiment at Windsor, in September, 1833, the king said that he hoped "that if ever they had to draw their swords it would be against the French, the natural enemies of England." This was a strange master for diplomatists to serve.

for Reform, the great Act had been looked forward to as the gate of entrance to a promised land where all things should be new and good. To following generations, who look back on the achievements of 1833 and 1834, these appear such as might amply satisfy the people with the ministry and Parliament of their choice. But it must be remembered that the country was then filled with vague and excessive hopes, such as bore in themselves the seeds of their inevitable disappointment. It was almost a political grievance that the devastations of the cholera, though beginning to abate, did not immediately disappear. There were, of course, many other evils which were capable of partial remedy by legislation and government, but even these partial remedies were of necessity slow in operation. Furthermore, the very magnitude and merit of the undertakings of the Reform ministry involved them in an honourable unpopularity. Every abolition of an abuse or a monopoly produced resentful discontent in some section of the people; and this discontent was, of course, in each instance keener and more active than such gratitude as might be diffused through the whole community. These causes were also not without similar effects within the ministry and the Cabinet itself. When so many great questions were touched, it could hardly be that individual opinions should not diverge, or that the group of men who had banded unanimously for the reform of the representative system, should continue to preserve that unanimity when reform was won. Stanley's difference from his colleagues on Irish matters, and especially on the disposition of ecclesiastical property, was the most pronounced, but by no means the only instance of this tendency to divergence. In a few cases it was augmented by personal peculiarities. Brougham and Durham were both in their several ways colleagues with whom it was often difficult to work. While Grey and Althorp remained at the head, their harmonizing influence restrained the divergent impulse, but it was already unmistakably present. Indeed, even Grey's presidency, though highly valued by the rest, seems to have often had an irritating effect on his somewhat unconciliatory son-in-law Durham.* Whatever discords there

---

* In December, 1831, Althorp wrote to his father, "We had a dreadful scene at my Cabinet dinner yesterday, which will probably lead to very detrimental consequences for the moment. Durham made the most brutal attack on Lord Grey I ever heard in my life, and I conclude will certainly resign. He will put this on the alterations in the [Reform] Bill—most unfairly, because there is no

might be in the Cabinet were not likely to be underrated by its depreciators in Parliament or in the press. And to the charge of divided counsels was added another, of want of skill and method in the ordinary administration of government. For this charge there would seem to have been some reason, and that not unnaturally. Until the Whigs came into power in 1830, they had been virtually excluded from office for nearly half a century, and the members of their ministry had had no training in the work of administrative government. At the same time, the greater part of them belonged to unprofessional and uncommercial classes, and were therefore almost equally without business training in their private occupations. Althorp himself, though conscientiously laborious in the work of his department, and with a very remarkable gift for arithmetical calculation, showed in occasional lapses his want of habituation to methodical affairs. Brougham wrote of him, "He was in essentials a good man of business, that is, he knew the cardinal points and acted on them, such as

alteration of any consequence in the main principle; and I doubt whether he knows anything about the alterations, as he will not allow anybody to tell him what they are." Greville gives a painful description of the scene after dinner, derived from the Duke of Richmond.

hearing all that people had to say, without either impatience or wish to censure ignorance, and yet not being quite silent, but both questioning enough and commenting a little, not deferring unless to leave undone what might do itself, doing only one thing at a time, and not breaking off improperly, nor yet being slow to change the subject, or be quickly occupied with the new one. But in numerous parts—the red tape parts—he was wholly and necessarily deficient. He had no care of his papers, for instance, and did not make his secretary take care of them; or if he did it was by chance."

In no department of government were the vague expectations of the public more embarrassing than in the department of finance, which was the especial concern of Althorp as Chancellor of the Exchequer. A Reformed Parliament, it was supposed, must bring a diminution of taxation. This was easier to demand than to effect. The preceding Government of Wellington had done its utmost to reduce expenditure; and when the Whigs came in there seemed small scope for further economy. Nevertheless, in the Budget which Althorp brought in, in April, 1833, he was able to show that in less than three years about three millions had been saved. The most satisfactory part of this economy was a saving of £230,000, effected by the abolition of thirteen hundred and eighty-seven sinecure or superfluous places. The total expenditure of the past year, estimated in the Budget of 1832 at £45,696,376, had actually amounted to only £45,366,000; and Althorp now counted on reducing it to £44,922,219 in the coming year. At the same time the revenue, estimated to yield £46,470,000, had actually yielded £46,853,000. These conditions made possible a decided, though not sweeping, diminution of the taxes. It was now proposed to abolish the duty on raw cotton (unwillingly permitted by Althorp in 1831), the house and window tax on shops, and the excise on tiles; and greatly to reduce the taxes on soap, on policies of marine insurance, and on advertisements. These reliefs would absorb about two-thirds of the estimated surplus of a million and a half, Althorp having cautiously allowed for a slight decrease in the revenue of the coming year.

He had selected for reduction those imposts which he thought most harmful to the industries of the country as a whole, and had done as much with each as his surplus seemed to allow. In the debate on the Budget it was allowed by Peel, and by the Opposition following Peel's lead, that the reductions could not have been carried further; indeed, Peel's only objection seems to have been that they were carried rather too far. But soon afterwards the disappointment of vague hopes outside the House found expression within it. The landed interest and the farmers were bent on a reduction of the malt tax. The townspeople were no less eager for abolition of the house and window taxes, or at least for a reduction of them much larger than that proposed in the Budget. The malt tax was first attacked. Since its reduction in 1822 to 2*s*. 7*d*. a bushel, or 20*s*. 8*d*. a quarter, it had remained stationary. Now Sir William Ingilby, a member for Lincolnshire, moved to reduce it by more than a half—from 20*s*. 8*d*. a quarter to 10*s*. By a combination of Tories and Radicals, and through apathy and negligence on the part of the supporters of the Government, Ingilby's motion was actually carried in a small House by 162 to 152. The Cabinet, and more especially the Prime Minister, thought the defeat so serious that they were on the verge of resignation, and only abandoned the idea on the urgent insistence of their supporters and of the king. The motion condemning the assessed taxes was still to come, but Althorp adroitly and boldly met it by action which not only repelled this attack, but also retrieved the former defeat. Sir John Key, a member for the City of London, moved for the repeal of the assessed taxes. Althorp moved an amendment that the deficiency of revenue which would be caused by the proposed reduction of the malt duty and abolition of the house and window taxes could not be compensated without the imposition of a general property and income tax, and by such recasting of the whole financial system as was for the present impracticable. This mention of the income tax does at once remind us that Althorp had already been its advocate many years ago; but he was still compelled to recognize that public opinion was unprepared for it, and this clause of his amendment was accepted as a truism by all parties without demur. The amendment was carried by 355 votes to 157, and the position of ministers in the House was thus re-established; but agitation outside against the assessed taxes continued some time longer. These taxes were a grievance of the townspeople, on whom they fell almost exclusively. Of nearly three million houses in Great Britain, less than one in every six was charged with house tax, and less than one in seven with window tax. The proposed exemption of shops and warehouses was complained of as insufficient, and the total abolition of the taxes was demanded. Sir John Hobhouse, who had just become Irish Secretary in Stanley's place, resigned, after much hesitation, both his office and his seat for Westminster, declining to help any longer to maintain these taxes against his own opinion and the strong desire of his constituents. He meant to retire from public life, but was persuaded to stand again for the vacancy he caused at Westminster. The Tory and the Radical party in the borough each put up a candidate, and Hobhouse lost the seat to the latter. In other parts of London and in some large towns the dislike of the taxes was angrily manifested, and in Clerkenwell there was serious rioting and loss of life. All this cost the Government popularity, which they could only hope to regain through the gradual recognition of the solid benefits which their labours were meantime securing to the country. Among their tasks affecting commerce and finance, two of the most important were the revision and renewal of the Charters of the East India Company and the Bank of England. The Bill dealing with the Indian Charter was in the hands of Charles Grant, the President of the Board of Control, and Hyde Villiers, the Secretary. Althorp had only a supervising influence on this weighty measure, which, besides its more important and imperial consequences, was a part of the general movement toward the abolition and restriction of monopolies, the especial work of the reformed representation. On the other hand, the Bill for the renewal of the Bank Charter was naturally in charge of the Chancellor of the Exchequer. In the preceding year he had procured the appointment of a committee on the subject, and although this committee had not presented a formal report, its labours had given him help enough to enable him to move his resolutions for the Bill on June 1, 1833. These showed that there was in the Government no pedantic jealousy of privileges as such, if they could be defended as existing for the public good and convenience. The privileges of the Bank Corporation were substantially renewed, and even substantially augmented by restraining all other banks, having more than six partners, from issuing notes or bills within sixty-five miles of London; also the notes of the Bank and its branches were made legal tender anywhere except at these banks themselves. On the other hand, there was to be no more secrecy in the administration of the directors of the Bank, but its control in the interest of the State was to be further secured by publicity.

The most noticeable point in the debates on this measure, in its bearing on Althorp's financial reputation, is the fact that when he proposed the recognition of bank-notes as legal tender he encountered the opposition of Peel, who protested that this would operate as a depreciation of the currency. But Althorp maintained and carried his proposal against Peel's great financial authority; and experience has proved that in this important fiscal calculation Althorp's judgment was the better of the two.

In surveying the first session of the Reformed Parliament, many of the discouragements and checks of the Liberal ministry seem now of very slight significance compared with that attributed to them at the time. Two fields of disappointment, however, stand out conspicuously, and with an intimate connexion in ill. These are Ireland and the House of Lords. The arduous and complicated work of incorporating the retarded civilization of Ireland in the commonwealth had received scanty attention from statesmen since the first step toward that end had been accomplished in the Act of Union. Much, indeed, had been done by natural causes—by commercial unity, by improved communication, and by the welding influence of the great French war. In service under the British flag, Irishmen of all ranks had learnt, like Scotchmen, to merge in a broader loyalty their undiminished attachment to their native island; and this double loyalty has been the glory of the best Irishmen ever since. On the other side, Englishmen began more and more to recognize the boon conferred by their high destiny in blending cognate but varying races with their own. But these natural causes of union had been almost unaided by legislative and administrative reforms, such as were then imperatively needful. At last the next great step was taken when the obstruction of one of the most contemptible of kings yielded tardily to justice and statesmanship, and the disabilities of Roman Catholics were swept away. Far more delicate and complicated, but not less necessary, was the work of reducing the legal but oppressive privileges of the ascendent Protestants in the island. It has been seen how the Liberal Government had now made its attempt to deal with these privileges in the Irish Church Temporalities Bill—an honest attempt, and probably quite as bold as public opinion would at that time allow. Then it was discovered that the House of Lords, though since the Reform Act it could no longer govern, had still the power of obstructing government, and was prepared to use that power. In many political questions, its judgment, even with its diminished responsibility, might still be fully as good as that of the House of Commons. Although certainly its wisdom was more likely to be of a conservative than of a reforming character, there might yet be privileges and monopolies which it would consent to abrogate, if they were such as it could decide upon without inevitable bias. But, in matters of Church and land, it was not to be expected that the Lords should be unbiased; and Irish questions were for the most part at the root questions of Church and land. Four times did the Lords refuse to pass clauses appropriating surplus Church revenues to unsectarian uses for Ireland, and for the time at least they prevailed. To overcome their obstruction the ministry had not here the great allies which enabled them to carry Reform. The people of Great Britain were only gradually and partially making up their minds to do full justice to their Irish fellow-citizens. And these lacked then, as ever, a worthy and commanding representative. There was no interpreting voice to speak for them with wisdom, firmness, and honest loyalty to the larger State. There have, indeed, been always, and now are, many patriotic Irishmen with these qualifications, but they have been invariably thrust to the background by those who have stooped to the appeals to party-spirit or to cupidity which their worthier countrymen despised. O'Connell, indeed, seems to have had impulses of humanity and patriotism, which often raised him much above the familiar wolfish pack of agitators, ever ready to tear open their country's wounds as soon as they begin to heal. Yet, if he cannot be charged with their hypocritical cruelty, he was not free from their selfish vanity or from their duplicity. He was never, indeed, compelled, as the present leader of Irish faction has been compelled, to confess that he had deliberately lied to the House of Commons; and it would be unjust to pronounce him capable of self-degradation such as this. But it is plain that he was generally distrusted by men who watched closely his action in Parliament and in the country. In 1835 Grey described him, in a letter to Melbourne, as "a man who means nothing but mischief for his own personal objects." Charles Greville calls him "an object of execration to all who cherish the feelings and principles of honour." Such as he was, however, he still retained the confidence of the great mass of Irish Catholics; a confidence only seriously impaired in the last years of his life, when his differences with the Young Ireland party, and disclosures of his conduct as landlord and middleman toward his tenants, together with other causes, displaced him from the position he had held so long. The Government had grounds for treating him as the spokesman of the majority in Ireland, but they had also grounds, which sometimes were forgotten, for exercising the utmost circumspection in so dealing with him. The grave consequences of this forgetfulness were to be remarkably illustrated in the ensuing year. At present he had acknowledged, often cordially enough, the efforts of the ministry toward Irish reforms, but with very little recognition of the real nature of the task before them, of its difficulties or of the means of overcoming them. When they were checked by one of the inevitable obstacles repeatedly encountered by them, he had recourse to a fitful clamour for Repeal of the Union, not really regarding this as feasible, and even conscious, very possibly, of its disastrous consequences to Ireland, but using it as a kind of vague threat to opponents. Opponents were strengthened by the clamour, and supporters alienated; counter-clamours were redoubled, and the voice of reason and justice had to wait for another interval to become audible.

But on the whole, notwithstanding the incompleteness of progress here and there, the first year of the Reformed Parliament had borne enough firstfruits of achievement to give good assurance that the great step taken in the preceding year was a step upward and not downward in the march of the nation through time. The abolition of slavery, the control of factory labour, the honest and careful, if imperfect, initiation of Church Reform in Ireland, the abrogation of legal abuses, and reduction of sinecures, had all set an honourable mark on the session of 1833. Next year a still weightier task was to be undertaken, an achievement of even more vital importance was to be accomplished, which would need all the vigour and resolution of Parliament and ministry alike, if they were to do their right work of carrying into effect the ideas of the wiser part of their fellow-countrymen. It was well that the new House of Commons had in one thing at least followed the tradition of its predecessor, in placing the same trust in the same man. It was well also that for one more year that man was to be left in the place which no other could fill so well; that it was under the leadership of his well-tried faithfulness and wisdom that the work of one more year was to be done.

CHAPTER VIII.

SECOND YEAR OF THE REFORMED PARLIAMENT.

DURING the recess that followed the session of 1833, Althorp had ample and weighty occupation in the preparation of measures to be brought forward by the Government next year. Of these measures, three had been committed especially to his charge—a Poor Law Bill, a Tithe Bill, and a Church Rates Bill. All were important, but the Poor Law measure was to be embodied in an Act as momentous and as salutary as was ever enrolled on the statute-book.

For many years the degrading pauperism of agricultural labourers had been the darkest cloud in the whole aspect of the condition of England. Political changes by themselves did nothing for these deep-seated evils; it was now to be seen whether they were to be allowed to remain unabated in mockery of the hardly won but barren triumph of Parliamentary Reform. Laws alone could, indeed, never create prosperity, however good they might be; but a change of bad laws could avert much needless wretchedness, and cut out a canker from the organic national life. This vital concern had not been forgotten by the ministry, even in the hottest part of the struggle for Reform. In 1832 they had appointed a Commission of Inquiry into the Poor Laws. The nine commissioners included Sturges Bourne, who had been Home Secretary in Canning's Government; Blomfield, Bishop of London; and Sumner, Bishop of Chester; but the most valuable and potent member of the commission was Nassau Senior. They were empowered to appoint assistant-commissioners, who were to conduct inquiries in every part of England and Wales. Among these assistants, again, the name of Edwin Chadwick, afterwards for thirteen years secretary to the first Poor Law Board, stands out as conspicuous for good work in the testimony of contemporaries. The interrogatories drawn up by the commission were both comprehensive and to the point; and the evidence thus obtained was valuable in quality as well as enormous in quantity. The assistant-commissioners, after inquiries lasting nearly a year and a half, returned their reports in January, 1833. Nearly a year more had passed before the commissioners could present their conclusive report, on which legislation was to be proposed. The report was anxiously deliberated by a committee of the Cabinet, of which Althorp was the principal member; and the charge of the new scheme was entrusted to him. It will be seen that, in Lord Russell's words, " the patience, the good sense, the practical experience, the unremitting labour, and the just influence of Lord Althorp overcame the obstacles which ignorance and prejudice interposed against this just measure."

The evils now proved to exist were no whit less gigantic than they had long been believed to be by those who had done their best to study the matter. Already a French commission had pronounced our corrupt poor-law system to be the political gangrene of England, equally dangerous whether it were meddled with or left alone. The worst evils were, indeed, of comparatively recent origin, for in the history of a people forty years are no long time; yet they were already so inveterate that it might well be feared, and many did fear, that they would be found irreparable. Through the seventeenth and eighteenth centuries the old Elizabethan law seems to have been not injuriously administered. It was the Act of 1796, allowing relief, almost unrestricted, to able-bodied "outdoor" paupers, and the reckless administration of that Act, which had all but severed the sinews of the manhood of the English poor. Through forty years the annual poor-rate had been steadily rising, until now it reached the sum of seven millions. This crushing tax was so wasted that, like all reckless doles, it was a curse to him who gave and to him who took. It was tossed out for the food of curs; in each man to whom it was seizable it sided with what was worst in him against what was best. It cut up by the roots the most elementary form of obligation—that from which philosophers have derived the primary evolution of a moral sense—the obligation of parents to maintain their offspring. The labourer was invited to put off that obligation on the parish, no less than the obligation to succour the old age of his father and mother. Support could be claimed, moreover, for illegitimate as well as legitimate children. Men and women were bribed to become vicious as well as helpless, and to be not only slavish paupers themselves, but to be the breeders of a slavish pauper brood. Meantime, those who squandered the rates to which they themselves contributed, were themselves also bribed by a delusive and disastrous gain. As they raised rates they lowered wages. Instead of employing an honest and independent labourer at a fair wage, they would employ a pauper at some far lower rate, to be supplemented from the parish tax. Under these conditions the independent labourer could hardly remain independent very long. He had to compete with the subsidized pauper; to choose between earnings on which he and his must starve, on the one hand, and joining the ranks of the pauperized on the other. Such a struggle could seldom be kept up long, and when, in Homer's phrase, "the day of slavery overtook him," it could seldom be that even "the half of his manhood" remained to him. The wonder is, not that so many sank, but that so many remained standing, and the resistance of even a few to the pestilent blast showed that there was still a core of manful and even heroic virtue among the English poor. In some few parishes also the administrators of the tax had struggled successfully against the corruption of the law and the custom. But such islands are hard to maintain unswallowed amid such a sea. The material effect of the system was as bad as the moral. All classes suffered detriment, however it might be disguised to some. Owners and tenants of land were crushed by the burden of the rates. The employer of labour paid, perhaps, no more in wages and rates together, than he would have paid if he had given fair wages without rates, or with only just rates. But in return he got incalculably worse labour. The total result was that the resources of the country, in money, goods, and human power, instead of being used in reproductive labour which would have multiplied and developed them, were absorbed in supporting an ever-increasing horde of plunderers.* It is not too much to say, in the words of a contemporary historian: "industry, probity, purity, prudence—all heart and spirit, the whole soul of goodness—were melting down into depravity and social ruin, like snow above the foul internal fires which precede an earthquake."

* Within the last few months died the Rev. H. P. Jeston, fifty-eight years vicar of a parish in Buckinghamshire, who gave valuable evidence before the commissioners. When he was appointed vicar in 1830, sixty-four persons out of ninety-eight who had a settlement in the parish were relieved from the poor-rate. This exceeded twenty-four shillings in the pound. Hence the glebe and all the land in the parish, except some sixteen acres, lay waste, and the relief was for some time paid out of rates in aid levied on other parishes in the hundred. After the enactment of the new Poor Law his parishioners steadily improved their condition, and at the time of his death not one was receiving pauper relief.

Such was the national calamity which the Reform ministry had resolved at last to face, and to achieve against it such defence as could be devised by law. The recommendations of the report of their commissioners might fairly be said to rise to the height of their great argument; and these recommendations the ministers resolved to carry out by means of the Bill which Althorp was to introduce. That some courage, as well as wisdom, was needed for the resolve, will appear later in relating the reception of the measure when it was disclosed. It accepted the principle, not unreasonably called Socialist, but recognized in England for two centuries and a half, that the destitute must be relieved by the community; that no man, woman, or child should be forced to die of want. But the Socialist principle was no longer to be allowed to work toward the ruin of the very class it should protect—the struggling and industrious poor. It was designed that relief, other than medical relief, to the able-bodied " outdoor " pauper, and allowances for his children, were to be discontinued as soon as possible. A poorhouse was to be within reach of all. Settlement by hiring and service was abolished: the only settlement to be recognized was that by birth or marriage. This was a gain not only to the liberty of the poor, but also to the community, which would profit by the improved facility for the circulation of labour. Illegitimate children were to be supported in most cases by their mothers. Within the poorhouse the able-bodied were to work ; the men were to be separated from the women, and the sick and infirm from the rest. Schools were to be provided for the pauper children ; a provision which, apart from its own merits, gave an impulse to national education in general, as it was felt that unpauperized children must not be left at a disadvantage in comparison with those of the workhouse schools. Finally, to carry out, maintain, and develop these principles, some of which must depend on administration rather than enactment, a new department of the central government was to be established under the name of the Poor Law Board. To this department were to be committed powers of control over the local administration of the poor-law to a degree almost unprecedented in English organization of the State. The Board was to consist of three commissioners, with twenty-one assistant-commissioners, to be reduced as soon as possible to nine. One of the most important offices of the

Board was to join together parishes into unions, and then to see that each union was provided with an adequate workhouse. This in itself was an immense gain in efficiency and economy. But besides this, the accounts, the diet, the discipline, the conduct of officials, were to be subject to constant inspection and supervision by the Board; whereby the condition of the pauper has from that time to this been steadily improved, without at the same time relaxing necessary precautions against its becoming too attractive to the poor.

Two months of the session were to elapse before Althorp could bring in this great measure, and in these months he had no lack of occupation and anxiety. The debate on the address in reply to the king's speech was noticeable for one of the very few pieces of incaution chargeable to Althorp during his whole tenure of office. It had been reported in a newspaper that an English member of Parliament, speaking to his constituents in the recess, had said that an Irish member, who had violently opposed the Disturbances Bill of last year, had privately urged the Government to carry it with all its provisions. On the first night of the debate on the address, O'Connell asked Althorp whether he or any other minister had made this statement. The answer was a negative, and would have been best without addition. But—partly, no doubt, from a wish to be fair to the English member in question, and partly from an impulse to express his own belief as to the truth, and his instinctive dislike of a want of frankness in any quarter—Althorp imprudently went on to say that he ought to add "that he had good reason to believe that some Irish members—certainly more than one—who had voted or spoken with considerable violence against the Bill, did in private conversation use very different language." By O'Connell's desire his followers began to rise in succession, each asking whether it were he. Then Althorp named Sheil as one of the members whom he had meant. Sheil denied the charge in the strongest terms. The feeling on the matter waxed warm, and the Speaker had to interpose. Even after the Speaker's interposition Althorp was provoked into intimating that, though he had undertaken to abstain from sending a challenge, he did not feel bound to decline one. He and Sheil were actually committed to the custody of the serjeant-at-arms; and when they were released, a committee of inquiry into the matter was appointed. Macaulay, who was one of the witnesses called, very rightly refused to give any report of private conversations; and though a certain amount of evidence was obtained, Sheil was acquitted of the charge. Althorp then withdrew it publicly, as a matter of course, expressing his regret to Sheil, with whom he had till then been on good terms. Sheil, indeed, who is described by Le Marchant as "a gentleman and a scholar, so that he seemed quite out of place among O'Connell's nominees," shared the general admiration of Althorp, felt much distaste for O'Connell's Parliamentary tactics and demeanour, and not long afterwards was offered and accepted office in the Whig Government. It was altogether an incident to be regretted, and Althorp cannot be absolved from the charge of indiscretion. But if he showed some imprudence in the affair, he showed also more magnanimity. A young member of the House, "of high character and position," had offered to prove the charge before the committee; but at the last moment, convinced by Macaulay's example and Abercomby's advice that private talk ought not to be thus brought up, he entreated Althorp to release him from his promise. This Althorp did, and took the consequent burden on himself. We may without much hesitation conclude that Sheil had really used the imputed language in unguarded talk, but had no less really forgotten it, and was honest in denying that he could recall it to his memory.

Within a fortnight of the opening of the session Althorp brought in his Budget—the last that he was to prepare, and the most successful. The popularity of Budgets generally depends more on the commercial prosperity of the country than on the greater or less skill of the Chancellor of the Exchequer of the day. The long depression of trade had in many quarters begun to pass away before the end of 1833. The value of exports had risen from just over thirty-six millions in 1832 to more than thirty-nine millions and a quarter in 1833. Textile manufactures—cotton, linen, wool, and silk—were all thriving vigorously, and the iron industries kept pace with them. The year before Althorp had calculated on a surplus of half a million; he was now able to announce it to be three times that amount. With this he proposed to abolish the house tax, of which the townspeople had expressed their dislike so strongly the year before, and to reduce the taxes on windows, on starch, and on some other articles of commerce. He proposed also a scheme for reducing the interest on 4 per cent. stock to $3\frac{1}{2}$ per cent., the success of which was an encouraging proof of confidence in his administration of the Treasury. In the revised financial statement which he introduced later in the session, he estimated the revenue at a little under forty-seven millions, the expenditure at a little under forty-five millions and three quarters. This expenditure included, it must be remembered, a charge of eight hundred thousand pounds for the interest on the twenty millions granted for the redemption of the West Indian slaves.

The representatives of agricultural constituencies grudged to the townspeople the relief they held due to their own industries, as they had shown emphatically the year before. In that year a Select Committee had been appointed to inquire into the causes of agricultural distress. That committee had indeed confirmed the general conviction of the existence of cruel distress in the agricultural parts of the country, but pronounced also that the best hopes of improvement "rested rather on the cautious forbearance than on the active interposition of Parliament." This did not satisfy the county members, and a week after the financial statement of 1834 was made, Lord Chandos moved that in any reduction of taxes due regard should be paid to the necessity of relieving the distress of the agricultural districts. His resolution was only defeated by 206 votes to 204. But when they descended from generalities to particulars, and from complaint to suggestion, the "agriculturists" could no longer maintain this formidable minority. Their only practical proposal was the repeal of the malt tax, a source of revenue yielding nearly five millions. This was moved by Sir William Ingilby, but he failed to show how the consequent deficiency of revenue could be satisfactorily supplied. Peel and most of the leading men of the Opposition declined to support the motion, and it was lost on a division by 271 votes against 170.

The true legislative means toward relief of agricultural distress were to be found in the Poor Law Bill about to be introduced by the Government. They kept that Bill steadily in view, and also the necessity of bringing it in as early as possible in the session, with a fair field before it. Otherwise it would have little chance of surmounting all the obstacles it was sure to encounter; and if it were not carried this year the opportunity might be lost for ever. To this end the English Tithe and Church Rate Bills, which Althorp had prepared with great labour and brought in amidst general approbation, were withdrawn. Two months were consumed in debates on the Budget, and in multifarious business and disputes. At last, on the 17th of April, Althorp rose in the House to set forth and plead for the provisions of the Poor Law Amendment Bill. It could not have been in better hands. Rhetoric was not needed, and would indeed have been out of place on a topic of so stern a gravity. The evidence collected by the commissioners spoke for itself, when ranged and summarized in clear and well-weighed words. The admonition to amendment, and the design of a great change, followed with inexorable cogency. The Commons felt in listening that the country was under the shadow of an appalling danger—a danger not less than that which had gathered round her in the armies of Napoleon. But they felt also that the plan for her defence now laid before them had come from men whose counsels might be trusted, whom duty bound them to follow and support. Of all those counsellors none could have greater weight with them than Althorp, even apart from his political leadership. The representative of a rural constituency, identified to the utmost with rural interests and feelings, conspicuous for his knowledge of the agricultural poor and active sympathy with them, one of the best-hearted, as well as most practical of men, he seemed by his earnest advocacy of the measure to give assurance of the real mercy of its sternness, a pledge that in its austere folds lay hidden a true germ of hope.

The almost unanimous tribute of honour and assent rendered to the Bill, on its introduction in the House by Althorp, was a true omen, happily, of its ultimate success. But it was not to be expected that its whole course should run smooth. It passed the second reading by a vote of 319 to 20, but in committee the inevitable attacks began. It offered an obvious opportunity to unscrupulous bidders for popularity, who could speciously represent it as an injury, not, as it really was, a help and encouragement to the struggling poor. It did, indeed, need supplementing by free importation of food, by an increased recognition of the right of workmen to combine freely for their own help, and by the increase of such self-reliant combinations themselves. Already there were formed here and there, and rapidly gathering power, those Trade Unions, which have, with all their defects, done more for the protection of labour than any State dole could do. But these were as yet very imperfectly organized and controlled, and a great deal of genuine apprehension of the consequences of limitation of poor-relief was joined, as is usual in such cases, with interested unscrupulousness. A great part of the newspaper press raised a declamatory outcry which very injuriously interfered with the fair trial of the new system throughout the country. But in Parliament, on the whole, the best men of all parties made fit and honourable renouncement of the spirit of party in dealing with this national reform. The Tories, indeed, could not but feel both that the local authorities cherished by them were about to be impaired and controlled, and also that a grave reproach to their party was implied, inasmuch as throughout their long term of power they had suffered dire evils to grow unchecked. It was but natural that they should be anxious to show, by criticism of the new proposals, the perplexing and many-sided nature of the problem, in excuse of their having shrunk from undertaking to solve it. But the criticism, however stringent, was criticism, not factious obstruction—at least from the leaders of the Opposition. Peel, rising above the smaller feelings, partly egoistic, partly partisan, into which he had somewhat lapsed during the struggle for the Reform Bill, gave a useful, though too unemphatic, support to the main provisions of the Bill. On the Radical side, the historian Grote, the unwearied advocate of the ballot, and also of all measures for improving the condition of the poor, came forward to second Althorp's motion for the first reading in a cogent and aptly worded speech. His support was invaluable, and rendered harmless the appeals to popular prejudice with which Disraeli, Cobbett, and sundry of the Radical party in the House declaimed against the Bill. After ample and stringent discussion in committee, it passed the third reading on the 1st of July, and went up to the House of Lords. There it was entrusted to the powerful conduct of Brougham, who, to his credit be it remembered, had been among the first to see the importance of the subject, and to promote the appointment of the commission and the legislative action on their report. The Bill found a support even weightier than Brougham's eloquent advocacy in the hearty and steadfast aid which Wellington, as might with assurance have been expected, rendered to its passage through the Lords. On the 21st of July it passed the second reading in that House by a large majority. In committee some amendments, chiefly affecting the bastardy clauses, which have since again been altered, were made. These were discussed, and, at Althorp's instance, accepted by the Commons with the least possible loss of time. On the 14th of August the royal assent was given, and the Poor Law Amendment Act became law.

The anxiety of its authors was relieved, but not ended, by its success in Parliament. It remained to be seen whether its work would justify it to its friends and foes. It could hardly be expected ever to attain to positive popularity; it was something better than popular, being salutary. At the same time, like all legislative dealings with social ills, it must be defective in flexibility and in reach, liable to abuse in administration, and fertile in disappointments. Yet for all this its good effects had begun to manifest themselves beyond dispute before a year was out; and each year of the following four confirmed its value. During that period good harvests and general prosperity helped its success; and in the harder times that followed, it had become too firmly established to be lightly shaken by renewed clamour. Some politicians and newspaper writers continued, indeed, to attack it with blind or malignant virulence. But facts were too strong for them. The poor-rates of

England and Wales, which in 1832 had been more than seven millions, had fallen in 1837 to but little above four. By that time we even find Althorp writing to Brougham from Northamptonshire, "So far as my observation goes, the new Poor Law is the most universally popular measure I can remember."

It was to be further observed that with the fall of rates had come also a rise of wages. Not only was the indigent ratepayer relieved of the cruel load which crushed him downward to the shame of receiving the rate he could no longer pay; but he and the rest of the labouring poor were now winning in honourable earnings what would before have come to them, if it came at all, in a degrading and paralyzing dole. The material and the moral succour given to them were, in fact, complementary and interdependent, and were more and more recognized by the people as a due and needful sequel to the Reform Act, that first decisive step toward the establishment of a democratic government in this country. It was a recognition of the poorer classes as an organic part of the living structure of the State, not as mere inorganic clay on which the rest might be reared. The system now superseded had, in fact, implied that indiscriminate massing together of those classes which is one of the most pernicious mistakes incident to a plutocratic form of government. It may doubtless be found also in connexion with communistic tendencies, but is of all things most alien to the healthier instincts of democracy. Few differences between men sharing a common humanity can really be much greater than that between the class which supplies able-bodied paupers and that which, by help of courage, diligence, self-control, and family affection, maintains an arduous independence, and often gives as strong proof as any higher layers of civilization can afford of the inextinguishable force and dignity of the soul. It is a due tribute of respect to the poor to discover and recognize their rights; it is a tribute no less due, and of still higher respect, to discover and recognize their duties.

Considered beside the Poor Law Amendment Act, the other incidents which made most stir in the session of 1834 seem now somewhat small and wearisome. These did, indeed, involve an actual change in the head of the ministry; yet the political significance of the confused blunders which led to the misadventure is nothing more than the old lesson that, as a chain is no stronger than its weakest link, so a group of men acting together is liable to disconcertment and defeat by the infirmity of any one member of it. In this case there were two such members, of whom one was Edward Littleton, the new Secretary for Ireland; and the misadventure occurred on a point of Irish legislation. It seems best, therefore, at this juncture briefly to review the Irish measures of the session.

The king's speech had invited the consideration of the House to a "final adjustment" of the vexatious question of Irish Tithe; and on the 20th of February Littleton brought in a Bill, of which the main feature was the commutation of tithe in Ireland into a land tax, redeemable after five years; at the same time the amount collected was to be reduced by a fifth. The Bill was generally regarded as inadequate and superficial, but it was read a first time, and the second reading fixed for the 2nd of May. Meantime O'Connell, who had been agitating outside the House for the Repeal of the Union, felt that he could no longer avoid bringing that question to an issue in Parliament. The form of doing this which he chose was a motion for a select committee to report on the means by which the Union had been effected, its operation in the past, and its probable consequences in the future. An opportunity was thus given of clearly setting forth the expediency and necessity of the Union, and the result was overwhelmingly decisive. The debate was continued for six nights, in which O'Connell and Spring Rice each spoke for a whole sitting of the House. Both their speeches are still worth reading, but might well have seemed somewhat unpractical encroachments on the time available in a busy session. Althorp, however, in the short speech with which he closed the debate, expressed his satisfaction with its length as at least showing an increasing interest in Irish affairs. Finally O'Connell's motion was rejected by 523 votes to 38.

Within a few days came the second reading of Littleton's Tithe Bill. The debate was signalized by two surprises—first the subdued and deferential tone suddenly adopted by O'Connell since his defeat on Repeal, and secondly an abrupt disclosure, or rather public accentuation, of the differences of opinion in the Cabinet. In speaking after O'Connell, Stanley appeared to Russell to have committed the Government to that opinion against the appropriation of revenues of the Irish Church to purposes of general benefit to the country which was the opinion held by Stanley and a minority of the Cabinet. Russell, therefore, thought it his duty to rise and assert, in opposition to his colleague, the right of Parliament to decide the manner of such appropriation. The issue was not allowed to drop, and a private member, Henry Ward, a cousin of the future Irish Viceroy, Lord Mulgrave, on May 27 moved a resolution for the reduction of the Irish Church Establishment, and for the application of the surplus to such uses as Parliament might determine. The motion was seconded by Grote, and while he was speaking, Althorp received news which made him rise to propose the adjournment of the House for six days. The news was that Stanley and Graham had resigned office—their first decisive step toward a secession to the Tory party, of which Stanley was afterwards to become the chief. With them went Ripon and Richmond. Spring Rice succeeded Stanley at the Colonial Office, and Lord Auckland took Graham's place at the Admiralty.

When the debate on Ward's motion was resumed, Althorp moved the previous question, announcing that the Government had decided on appointing a commission of inquiry. This decision had been accepted by Althorp and Russell as a step toward educating public opinion to the principle of Appropriation. Stanley joined with the extreme Tories on the one hand, and with O'Connell and his party on the other, in objecting to the issue of the commission. Peel, on the contrary, with the more responsible Tories, was inclined to favour it. Althorp's motion was carried by 396 to 120. Meantime, however, the king had added to the embarrassment of his ministry by an ill-considered and tearful speech to a deputation of Irish bishops, in which he talked of his duty and resolution to protect the rights of the Established Church of Ireland. His brother, the Duke of Cumberland, a fanatic Orangeman, asseverated in the House of Lords that he never could or would consent to any alienation of the property of the Church. It was well that the Duke of Cumberland's consent could be of no importance to the country so long as the Princess Victoria, then heiress to the throne, should be alive. Once more in the session the question of Appropriation was raised, when, in committee on the Irish Tithe Bill, O'Connell, on the 23rd of June, moved an instruction to the committee that whatever surplus should be left, after due provision had been made for the wants of the Church, should be applied to purposes of charity and education; and with this Althorp and Russell both expressed their agreement. But the opposition of the House of Lords was persistent, and prevented any real advance in this direction for many years to come.

Another Irish question, and that a pressing one, with which the ministry had to deal, was the continuance of turbulence and certain kinds of violent crimes in various parts of the island. These had considerably abated since the Disturbances Act of the year before, which had so divided the Cabinet, had been passed. But the Act, after the ill-advised fashion habitual with Acts of the kind, was to expire after a fixed period; in this case the period was a year. Some similar Act would plainly be necessary, but it was to be considered whether it would be possible to omit some provisions of the last Act. It was now that the disastrous idea seems to have entered into the minds of the Lord Chancellor and the Irish Secretary that some sort of influence on the attitude of O'Connell might be obtained by means of concession to the views he professed as to the need of certain of these provisions. There were clauses especially objected to by him which gave power to the Lord-Lieutenant to prohibit public meetings. But Lord Wellesley, Wellington's elder brother, the distinguished Governor-General of India, who had succeeded Anglesey in the Lord-Lieutenancy, had come to the conclusion that these clauses must be retained, though others establishing courts-martial might be omitted, in the new Bill for the Suppression of Disturbances. Wellesley had definitely made this recommendation in a letter on the 11th of June. On the 19th Littleton and Brougham each wrote to Wellesley, urging him to consent to the abandonment of the clauses on public meetings for the sake of facilitating the Parliamentary management of the Government, and to write again in this new sense to the Prime Minister. Not only did they despatch these letters without consulting their colleagues, but even next day when the Cabinet met, and the subject was discussed, Brougham made no mention there of what he and Littleton had done, but acquiesced in the proposal to re-enact the clauses. Three days afterwards Grey was astonished to receive a letter from Wellesley, which, in Grey's words, "in direct opposition to Wellesley's own strongly expressed opinion on the 11th," announced his willingness to dispense with the clauses in question. On the same day Littleton also received a letter to the same effect from Wellesley. This he showed or reported to Althorp, who came to the conclusion that, after this distinct recommendation of the Lord-Lieutenant to drop the clauses, it would be impossible to ask Parliament to renew them, and that the decision of the Cabinet on the 20th must therefore be reversed. Littleton went on to press for permission to use this opportunity for disarming the hostility of O'Connell without delay. It was known that O'Connell was planning new agitation in Ireland—agitation which might lead to disorder or the loss of a seat at a coming election for Wexford. Would it not be well—such was Littleton's contention—that O'Connell should know that the clauses on public meetings, which formed one of his chief grievances, might after all not be proposed—at least that the form of the Bill was not yet fixed? O'Connell's knowing this in time might save a great deal of friction in the administration of Irish affairs. On this appeal, Althorp, in his own words in Parliament afterwards, "saw no harm in this, if it went no further; but he begged Mr. Littleton to be extremely cautious, and not to commit himself." Althorp's trust in the discretion of the Chief Secretary was misplaced. Littleton used the permission, but forgot the accompanying condition. He allowed the wily O'Connell to elicit from him the fact that Wellesley had recommended the omission of the clauses, and even that Althorp had thought the recommendation conclusive. Littleton promised that when the Cabinet had decided, he would let O'Connell know. He seems to have thought that his indiscretion was redeemed by exacting from O'Connell, whose character he might by that time have known, a pledge of his honour to complete secrecy.

Meantime the Prime Minister had written back to Wellesley, expressing astonishment at his change of mind, and received a private letter in reply, which plainly established that his suggested suggestion of omitting the clauses would not have been made if he had regarded only the facts within his view in Ireland. The Cabinet met again on the 29th of June, when Grey produced this letter. Althorp, who had come with his mind made up to omit the clauses, was taken aback by this change of Wellesley's attitude, but on the whole felt bound to regard in preference the Lord-Lieutenant's formally expressed readiness to govern without the clauses. He was opposed, as he expected, by Grey, but was astonished and somewhat disgusted to find that Brougham had now turned round, and strongly advocated these clauses, the omission of which he had originally suggested. Althorp held to his argument, and divided the Cabinet on the question, but was in a minority. The same evening, after going home, he wrote Grey a letter which was virtually a resignation. In great distress the Prime Minister wrote back at once, pleading earnestly against his threatened secession, involving inevitably a break-up of the Government ; and followed up the letter by repeated interviews, in which Althorp's feelings could not but be strongly moved by the appeals of his venerable chief. He found, too, that all the rest of the Cabinet, whether siding with him on the disputed point or not, looked on it as a matter of detail, not of principle ; and certainly the vacillating conduct of the Lord-Lieutenant greatly impaired the clearness of the issue. At last Althorp consented to remain, and on the evening of the 1st of July, the Suppression of Disturbances Bill, moved by Grey, was read the first time in the House of Lords. All this time neither Althorp nor any other minister had been told by Littleton of his unauthorized communication to O'Connell. Nor did Littleton resign when he found the clauses retained. O'Connell also remained quiet all the day after the Bill was introduced; then, on the 3rd of July, he rose in the House and proclaimed aloud the communications made to him by Littleton, which he had promised to keep secret faithfully. These he made the ground of an accusation against Grey of misrepresenting the recommendations of the Lord-Lieutenant, and against Althorp of consenting to clauses which he disapproved. Littleton replied with indignant severity on O'Connell's breach of faith, but acknowledging his own disastrous indiscretion with bitter regret. Next day he tendered his resignation, but it was three days too late to be of service to himself, and was equally useless to the ministry. At the request of his chiefs he withdrew it, while they considered their collective action. On the 7th of July Althorp, whose whole conduct towards Littleton was, in the latter's own words, characterized by great magnanimity, came forward at his urgent request to defend him to the utmost extent compatible with truth. The Secretary for Ireland, Althorp said, had stated with perfect truth to O'Connell that the Cabinet had not yet decided the question of retaining or omitting the clauses. Littleton was satisfied with this defence; but, apart from his communication to O'Connell, he had erred in joining Brougham in his plan of making suggestions to Wellesley undisclosed to their colleagues; nor was Wellesley justified in adopting the suggestions against his own judgment. It now seemed that the burden of excusing these faults also was about to be laid on Althorp. Notice was given of a motion for the production of the private correspondence between members of the Government in England and Ireland. This might fairly have been rejected as an unwarrantable breach of privacy, and the Government had been assured of a majority by defeating a motion of O'Connell's for a select committee on certain Irish papers by 157 votes to 73. But this did not satisfy Althorp. The views of the Lord-Lieutenant might reasonably be asked for by the House, and they could not be explained without either leaving open to censure, or else attempting to justify, Littleton, Brougham, and Wellesley. It was equally repugnant to Althorp to abandon the defence of colleagues and to maintain it against his conscience. The same night he wrote to tell Grey that it was impossible for him in these circumstances to conduct the Bill through the House, and that he must finally resign. Again the Prime Minister besought him long and earnestly to withdraw his resignation, but this time in vain. The same course remained inevitable for Grey. Now less than ever could he conscientiously adopt Althorp's original proposal to omit the clauses. But without Althorp by his side in the ministry he could neither carry through this Bill nor, he believed, carry on the government of the country. On the 8th of July he received Althorp's final reply to his expostulations; on the 9th he announced to the House of Lords, in noble and touching words, his own resignation, and the end of his beneficent and illustrious public life.

On the same evening Althorp announced in the House of Commons the dissolution of the ministry, preserving in his statement the same reticence as before on the subject of the indiscretions of his colleagues. But when the Lord Chancellor had the assurance to write reproaching him with breaking up the Government, making no reference to Brougham's own share in the disaster, even Althorp's patience was moved to reply in an outspoken, though still most kindly and good-tempered, private letter. As this letter gives the truth of the matter concisely, it seems worth while to quote it at length.

"Downing Street, July 10, 1834.

"MY DEAR BROUGHAM,

"I admit that I am answerable as the proximate cause of the dissolution of the Administration, but the situation in which I was placed was not by any act of my own. I wish you would look a little at the share you have taken in the business. Without communication with one of your colleagues, with the view, I know, of facilitating business in Parliament, you desired Littleton to write to Lord Wellesley, and you wrote to him yourself, to press him to express an opinion that the three first clauses of the Bill might be omitted. He did express that opinion, and I thought, and still think, that when the Lord-Lieutenant of Ireland said that any circumstance of expediency would induce him to carry on the government of that country by the ordinary law, to whatever extent he made that admission it was the duty of the Government here to agree with him. He had said he did not want the court-martial clauses; we properly omitted them. He then said he could go on without these three clauses, and I think we ought to have omitted them also; but you, having originally produced the difficulty by writing to Lord Wellesley, gave your decision directly against what you had advised Lord Wellesley to do. The consequence of all this was that I got placed in a position which rendered it impossible for me to go on. This impossibility was mainly produced by Littleton's communication to O'Connell, but even without this the difficulty was likely to be enormous.

"I am aware that the man who by his resignation produces the dissolution of an Administration takes a great load upon his shoulders, and more especially when there is so much difficulty in forming another; this load is increased greatly when he cannot explain the causes which compelled him to take such a step without involving others, whom for every reason he is determined not to involve. That load I must bear; but it never can compel me to support measures which I disapprove, though, if no other than a Tory Government can be formed, it may render it incumbent on me not to give them a factious opposition.

"Yours most truly,
"ALTHORP."

The dismay of the Liberals at the resignation of their two chiefs was naturally great; and it extended among all sections of the party, even those which had given the ministry the most uncertain support. It was felt that Grey was irrevocably gone, but that a great effort must be made to do everything possible to recover Althorp. Within four days of his resignation two hundred and six members of the party in the House of Commons had signed and presented to him an address, expressing their desire of his return to office, and promise of faithfully supporting him there. As soon as the address was hurriedly presented, it was found that even a larger number of members would have joined in it if it had been made known to them. "Such a demonstration," Mr. Walpole observes in his History, "had perhaps never previously been presented to any public man." Lord Essex wrote of Althorp to his father on the 11th of July, "Surely he might take the Premiership, if only for the end of the session? It seems to be every one's wish, yet I fear he will not consent. . . . I do trust that he may be persuaded to remain; every one is crying out for his doing so, and all will be right if he will."

Meantime the country was for a few days without an Administration. The king would have willingly accepted a Tory Government, but was soon convinced that this was at present impossible. He then suggested a coalition ministry, with a Liberal, Melbourne, at its head, but including Wellington and Peel. This also Melbourne considered impossible, and went on to tell the king that he could only undertake to form an Administration on one condition—that it should be joined by Althorp. Grey concurred in thinking this essential, and yet again joined his entreaties to those of the king and Melbourne, and of all Althorp's colleagues, followers, and friends, to persuade him to take up once more the burden that he had just laid down. So long as it was possible, he withstood those entreaties altogether. At last he was induced to refer the matter to three eminent Liberal members of the House, intimate friends of his own, Ebrington, Tavistock, and Bonham Carter. They pronounced unanimously that if his views on the Suppression of Disturbances Bill were accepted he had no justifying ground for refusing to serve again. Then he yielded his consent, making only one more stipulation, that Littleton should return to his office; "a noble act"—thus Littleton himself described it—"dictated by a fine sense of honour, and wholly unexpected by me." Gladly would Melbourne and all the other ministers have served under Althorp as Prime

Minister, even as Grey had desired to serve in 1830; but to this he again refused consent, and resumed his old office of Chancellor of the Exchequer. Lord Duncannon succeeded his brother-in-law Melbourne at the Home Office, and Hobhouse took Duncannon's place at the Woods and Forests, with a seat in the Cabinet. By the middle of July the ministry was reconstructed. On the 18th of the month Essex wrote again enthusiastically to Althorp's father, "What an angel is your son! He has saved his king and country by sacrificing all his own feelings for the public good, and he must reap the reward such conduct deserves from a generous people. Lady Grey said to me yesterday morning, 'Of all the persons now to be admired in this world, is Lord Althorp; never was anything like it.' This is the general feeling."

The Irish Bill, amended by the omission of the disputed clauses, now passed smoothly through the House. It was to be only in disturbed districts proclaimed by the Lord-Lieutenant that unauthorized meetings were to be illegal, or that carrying arms or being abroad between sunset and sunrise were to be offences under the Act. The Bill was read the first time on the 18th of July, and the third time on the 26th. Early in August it had passed the Lords; and during the year for which it was law no ill consequences followed, to Althorp's great relief, from the omission of the clauses to which he had objected. Littleton's Irish Tithe Bill was less fortunate. The collection of tithe as a land tax, to be afterwards distributed by the State among the clergy and tithe-owners, was in itself unsatisfactory, and was obscured by somewhat cumbrous complications. On the 30th of July, when it was in committee, O'Connell, in a small House, carried by 82 votes to 33 an amendment that the tithes should be reduced 40 per cent., and made payable immediately from the landlords to the clergy. The Government accepted the amendment, but the Lords threw out the whole Bill by 189 votes to 122, thereby making the ultimate disendowment and disestablishment of the Irish Church more inevitable than before, and for the present emphasizing once more the obstruction of the Upper House to measures of Irish Reform.

On the 14th of August the Poor Law Act, the great work of the session, received, as we have seen, the royal assent; and on the next day Parliament was prorogued. The House of Commons rose, glad at Althorp's restoration to his old place, and looking on to being led by him again when they should meet next year. This was not to be; the members of that House had listened for the last time to the manly, unstudied utterance of his wise and honest words. His father, now in the seventy-seventh year of his age, had greatly failed in health during the last part of the session, adding thereby to Althorp's anxieties, and during the autumn sank rapidly. On the 10th of November he died, and Althorp succeeded him in his peerage as the third Earl Spencer. He was thus, of course, irrevocably exiled, by one of the most untoward, and sometimes highly mischievous, of our constitutional customs, from the political field where he could best serve his country, and where his presence or absence might perhaps yet make, as it had made before, an incalculable difference in some crisis of national history. One difference it made immediately, creating no small stir at the time, though in its ultimate effect it was of comparatively small moment. William the Fourth paid Althorp the superfluous and unwelcome tribute of considering his loss in the Commons so fatal to the Government that it behoved the king to call for the resignation of his ministers, and to invite Wellington to form a Tory Administration. Melbourne had gone down to Brighton to consult the king as to the fittest successor to Althorp's leadership of the Commons; he returned the next day bearing this singular and unexpected message to the duke. It appears, indeed, from a letter written on the 12th of November by the Prime Minister to the king, and lately made public for the first time, just fifty-five years afterwards, in the volume entitled "Lord Melbourne's Papers," that it was Melbourne who made the initiative suggestion to the king of the possibility that the loss of Althorp in the Commons might be insuperable. This letter, dated two days after Lord Spencer's death, says, "The Government in its present form was mainly founded on the personal weight and influence possessed by Earl Spencer [Althorp] in the House of Commons. That foundation is now withdrawn, and in the new and altered circumstances it is for your Majesty to consider whether it is your pleasure to authorize Viscount Melbourne to make such fresh arrangements as may enable your Majesty's present servants to continue to conduct the affairs of the country, or whether your Majesty deems it advisable to adopt any other course." Thus the king's consequent action, however injudicious and hasty it may have been, was not quite so unconstitutional as it appeared at the time and has generally been considered since. But whatever excuse there may have been for it, at any rate it had little effect beyond causing much needless inconvenience to all concerned. In less than five months Melbourne and a Liberal ministry were in power again, with six years of government before them. But the best-beloved of the Liberal chiefs had bidden his final farewell to political office. From the time of his father's death the new Lord Spencer had been maturing a resolution to retire from active political life, and before the next session of Parliament opened in February, 1835, he had definitely announced this resolution in letters to several friends and supporters. His retirement was caused by personal inclination and by a conviction of private duty, both working the same way; but it was the latter motive which determined him decisively. He had long been aware that his father lived extravagantly, keeping up large establishments not only at Althorp and Spencer House, but also at his place on his Wimbledon property, and lavishing money on collections of curiosities, on profuse hospitality, and in many other ways only befitting men who have little cause for thrift. He had once at least talked to his son of retrenchment, but had done nothing. Althorp, whose intercourse with him was constantly affectionate, had answered these transient compunctions with his usual self-sacrificing generosity. He could not bear that his parents should be distressed in their old age by a change in their way of living. He desired that the burden of retrenchment should fall on himself, who "had no desire to keep up the state of a great nobleman, and was prepared," so he wrote to his father, "to live very economically until the mortgages you have contracted can be discharged." He was prepared to bear the burden, whatever it might be, but did not then know how heavy he was to find it. At his father's death he made painful discoveries of the recklessness with which the property had been encumbered. He could now, he said, "only regard himself as the nominal owner of his patrimony." But he made no complaint against the dead, and with characteristic cheerful patience addressed himself to the lifelong task of doing for the sake of a brother and a nephew what his own father could not bring himself even to attempt for the sake of a noble and devoted son.

His retirement was not acquiesced in without repeated and earnest remonstrance from his colleagues. Melbourne, whom he had warned before of the probability of his withdrawal from public life, wrote to him the day after Lord Spencer's death, to beg him "not to come to any hasty unalterable determination" on the matter; and three days later Charles Wood (Grey's son-in-law, afterwards Lord Halifax) urged him, in a loyal and earnest letter, "to consider in how different a position all those would feel themselves who looked up to him as their natural leader," and "for the sake of his friends and followers not to leave them headless." "We all," Wood wrote, "feel safe and right so long as you are a member of the Government; but so chief a stone being left out of the wall would shake the whole fabric." Next year, when the brief interpolated term of Peel's administration was over, and the Whigs were again in office, these solicitations of old colleagues were renewed. Melbourne, now again Prime Minister, wrote, pressing him to join the Cabinet in terms not less urgent than those of his letter of November. Once more the appeal was made without success. The champion whose aid his old followers sought would have been shorn of half his strength in the unfamiliar and uncongenial chamber in which his newly inherited rank imprisoned him; and even without regarding this crippling change, the prerogative claims of private duty might well, as we have seen, be deemed by him to be exclusively engrossing. From time to time, during the remaining ten years of his life, he came forward to use his great political authority on behalf of principles and measures which seemed to demand some utterance from him on their behalf; but this he did always henceforward as a private citizen, speaking for himself alone. His wearisome burden of office, borne patiently and faithfully during four crowded and arduous years, had been now finally laid down.

CHAPTER IX.

RETIREMENT AND LAST YEARS.

In a very short fragment of an autobiography, begun about this time by the new Lord Spencer, but either abandoned abruptly or else almost entirely lost, he wrote, "I am told I shall feel the want of political excitement, and be unable to find employment for my time. I do not think those who tell me this know my character; I believe that the pursuits which I followed in my country life before I came into office would be sufficient for my happiness now." In writing thus he showed no less self-knowledge than Melbourne had done when he wrote a little earlier, shortly after yielding his place to Peel, "I was never happier than now, but I suppose I shall soon be damned tired of doing nothing, as all are on leaving office."

The ex-Chancellor of the Exchequer had always stood alone among public men (unless when they feel great physical exhaustion or mental disappointment) in maintaining a dislike of office, which no relief from it, however long, could overcome; nor had he any lack of things to do in his retirement. A large part of his occupation was, as has been shown, the austere task of repairing the crippled fortunes of his house by rigorous retrenchment and self-denial. Not only Spencer House, but even Althorp itself, was virtually shut up, a few rooms only being reserved for the visits of the master, and now and then a few near relatives or intimate friends. He lived in his old home as an agent or a steward, and a steward from whom he exacted a strict account. The deer were given away to friends, the park in which they had roamed being assigned to the grazing of more profitable occupants. The garden was let to the gardener, who kept it up and made his necessary profit by selling the fruit, vegetables, and flowers. In a letter written in 1836, this frugal earl mentions incidentally that he must consider the cheapest mode of returning from Scotland, and has decided to travel by a steamer from Dundee to Hull. He spent most of his time at Wiseton, the place which had come to him through his wife. Here he had spent much of his short married life, and here he kept the farm which was the principal field of his experiments in agriculture and stock-breeding. These were to him an interest at once exhilarating and seriously important. He would do all that was in his power to help his country to maintain a leading place in the progress of the ancient arts of husbandry and pasturage. On these matters he constantly wrote and conferred with such eminent agriculturists as John Grey of Dilston, manager of the Greenwich Hospital estates in Northumberland, or Lord Leicester, or the Duke of Richmond, with whom he joined in the movement which resulted in the establishment of the Royal Agricultural Society. Of that society he was afterwards an honoured and efficient president. He won the highest prizes with his shorthorn cattle, and his sheep were but a little way behind. Anecdotes abound of his love of his herds and flocks. An old shepherd on the Althorp estate told a friend of his master how he would seat himself on the grass to watch the long flock as they went slowly by beside him, and would know each several sheep as though, said the old man, "he had lived with them." When efforts were being made to induce him to become a member of the ministry in the spring of 1835, his friend and former secretary,

Thomas Drummond, came down to Althorp with a final petition from Melbourne and his colleagues that he would join them. He was at the window, gazing at the lately born lambs beside their mothers, and when he had listened to the message he turned again and pointed to them in the pasture, declaring that with them he must remain.

George Ticknor, the American traveller and author of a "History of Spanish Literature," met him at Wentworth in the autumn of 1835, and has recorded his first impressions of this meeting. He describes him as "short and thick-set, with a dark-red complexion, black hair beginning to turn grey, a very ordinary farmer-like style of dress, and no particularly vivacious expression of countenance. His manner was as quiet and simple as possible. He does not talk brilliantly—hesitates and even blushes." Next day his further conversation, especially a clear and powerful exposition of the Poor Law, showed Ticknor something of what this modesty and homeliness concealed. His bodily strength and capacity of endurance, though not what it had been before his exhausting labours in office, were still considerable. Ticknor mentions his riding one day to Wakefield and back in the rain, a ride of thirty-six miles.

His life was thus mainly outdoor and practical; but that his mind dwelt often on spiritual and intellectual concerns is shown not only by the testimony of friends, but by long and numerous letters, in which he discusses, not with any novelty of philosophic suggestion, but with no inconsiderable reasoning power and discernment, such subjects as the Immateriality of the Soul, the difference between Reason and Instinct, and the like. Brougham, who was his chief correspondent on these matters, dedicated to him a treatise on "Natural Theology," and in the dedication spoke with great respect of his studies in this kind, even expressing a hope that they might be published. This was not likely; he had not given up politics for philosophy, but for the other alternative of his favourite poem;

> "Rura mihi et rigui placeant in vallibus amnes,
> Flumina amem silvasque inglorius."

Although his withdrawal from official political life was final and complete, he was not the man to be guilty either of the affectation of despising politics, or of such want of public spirit as would have declined whatever opportunities of action were compatible with the elected tenor of his life. From anything like interference with the administration or patronage of a government for which he was no longer responsible, he most scrupulously abstained. The only exception, as he himself calls it in a letter to Spring Rice, was his suggestion that his private secretary and intimate friend, Thomas Drummond, should be entrusted with the important post of Under-Secretary in the Irish Administration. The appointment was made, and abundantly justified by Drummond's devoted and admirable discharge of his trust. Spencer wrote of him in the letter mentioned above, "I am delighted to see his appointment, because I think it impossible for you to have selected another man so good for the place; he has, in addition to the first class of abilities, a perfect temper (I have known this from having lived in the same house for three years), and one of the most honourable and conscientious minds I ever met with. Both these last are inestimable in Ireland." Except in this more than justifiable instance, he neither asked office for others nor would accept it for himself, even when it would have been held in new fields demanding no return to Downing Street. In November, 1838, Melbourne pressed him to take either the Lord-Lieutenancy of Ireland or the Governorship of Canada, but he declined both. His refusal of the Canadian post, however, was only decided on after serious reflection. " With respect to Canada," he wrote to Melbourne, " there is, I think, a balance of duty, and, as I told you at Windsor, I very seriously considered what it was my duty to do. I told you the result of that consideration, and afterthoughts have not induced me to change my opinion. To go without hoping to be successful would, of course, be absurd, and success would, as I told you, involve the necessity of my residence in Canada for so long a time that at my age I must consider it banishment for life. I should, therefore, by going abandon every private duty which I am now endeavouring to perform; I should sacrifice the probable hope of being able to do a less good for the very distant possibility of doing a greater. I am quite aware that we are all of us inclined to overrate the importance of the pursuits in which we are engaged, and I dare say, therefore, that I overrate the good I may be able to do in my present pursuits; but still I think I am doing some good. Whatever this is, I must sacrifice it; but much beyond this, I must sacrifice every private duty as a relative, as a neighbour, and as a country gentleman, which I am now able to perform. I must, therefore, now decline to accept this more formal offer, as I did before the less formal one which you made me."

But toward the close of the Whig Administration there were questions absorbing more and more of public attention on which he could not remain politically inactive. These were the questions of the Repeal of the Corn Laws, and of the carrying out of the principles of Free Trade in general. Both as a financier and as an agriculturist he felt bound to declare his convictions on the subject. He made the inclination of the Melbourne ministry toward Free Trade a reason for coming forward to commend his old colleagues in moving the address in the House of Lords, when they were already virtually dismissed from office by the adverse general election of the summer of 1841. He watched with satisfaction the fiscal reforms of Peel and Goulburn, many of which he would himself have carried out if he had been as resourceful and masterful as Peel, and, still more, if public opinion, the lord of financiers, had been as ripe for those reforms in his time as in Peel's. But on the great question of the Corn Laws he was far in advance of Peel, and this notwithstanding much that would have biased most men to the other side. He was both a landowner and a farmer, and convinced that a serious fall in the price of corn "would leave him without an income." He did not think, however, that the fall in price caused by free importation would be nearly so great as was expected, and at any rate held that the risk ought to be faced by himself and his class for the common weal. In 1841 he wrote that he still thought "the Corn Laws popular in the country as a whole," although, as he says in another letter of the same year, "so long as they are maintained the country is on the edge of a precipice." His convictions waxed stronger each year, and also his cheerful hope that the repeal of the laws would, by general encouragement of industry, prove ultimately to be for the benefit of agriculturists as well as of the whole State. In December, 1843, at a civic dinner at Northampton, he delivered a speech emphatically announcing his convictions on this matter. "This speech," says Sir Denis Le Marchant, "though now well-nigh forgotten, created at the time a sensation almost without parallel throughout the whole country; it was copied into every newspaper, and was unquestionably the death-note of the Corn Laws, being followed by an address from

Lord John Russell to his constituents in the form of a letter strongly advocating the same line, and ultimately by the measures taken in Parliament by Sir Robert Peel."

A year and a half after this he made his last speech in Parliament, in support of Peel's Maynooth College Bill, which was to be read a second time in the House of Lords in June, 1845. He welcomed the measure as the earnest of a more liberal spirit towards the Irish Roman Catholics, now gradually overcoming that spirit of "Ascendency" which he had always combated and condemned. He took up the phrase of an opponent peer who complained that the Protestant Church in Ireland had not fair play, and in his own sense adopted it, showing that Protestantism could not indeed have fair play while it was given an invidious and factitious predominance. "I hope," he said, "this is not an isolated measure. I hope and trust that you are prepared to pursue a different policy towards Ireland; and if you do so, I trust you will not only confirm the Union with Ireland, but render that country, by a proper and steady system of conciliation and liberality, the strength instead of the weakness of the empire." Words and phrases which on the lips of most politicians are often little more than hackneyed commonplaces, came from him with heartfelt reality; and this, his last public utterance, was the expression of his earliest and most vivid political motive, the abhorrence of religious intolerance.

His life was now drawing near its close. In the summer of 1843 he had been talking to a friend of his plans for the future; and after describing what he meant to do in the year following, he added with perfect calmness, "And the year after that I shall die." This strange prescience remained constantly with him, though there were no apparent grounds for it. He continued his active habits, yielding them only gradually to the advance of age. In diet he erred by an excess of abstinence. He seems to have had as great a horror of hereditary gout as of hereditary debt. "He used to weigh his breakfast, and then, having eaten the very small portion he allowed himself, rush half famished from the room to escape further temptation. Nothing but his great power of self-denial could have enabled him to persevere in a mode of life so trying, and, in all probability, really injurious." In the autumn of 1845, in the sixty-fourth year of his age, his prediction was fulfilled. He was taken ill suddenly at Doncaster, toward the end of September, and was with difficulty taken home to Wiseton. There it shortly became manifest that he was dying. The day before his death he finished all arrangement of affairs with his brother and successor, and insisted that he should not give up his rest to watch that night. In his last hours his thoughts were neither of politics nor of the private duties he had so faithfully discharged, but of the young wife whom he had lost twenty-seven years ago. He was one of those bereaved who can say truthfully to lost wife or husband—

> " No later light has lightened up my heaven,
> No second day has ever dawned for me;
> All my life's bliss from thy dear life was given,
> All my life's bliss is in the grave with thee."

His wife's place had never been filled either in his house or in his heart, and those who knew him best knew that his old sorrow lived on unquenched beneath his genial serenity. Now he asked for a locket enclosing a lock of her hair, which he had promised her to wear when he should die; and having put this round his neck, he awaited death with calm and even gladness. He had cherished the sure faith of a Christian in the life of the world to come, and believed that he was now on the eve of reunion with the lost, and of some new happiness even greater than the old. About five in the morning of the 1st of October the life of his body became extinct; and it was buried, according to his desire, with complete privacy and simplicity, in the grave where long ago he had laid the body of his wife.

CHAPTER X.

RETROSPECT AND PROSPECT.

ALTHORP'S place in the history of his country is far less conspicuous than it is important. It has been seen how indispensable was his leadership in the momentous struggle for Reform, and during the two years that followed it; years at least as illustrious for beneficent legislation as any other two in all the historic centuries of the mother of Parliaments. In these pages reference has more than once been made to the frequent and emphatic testimony of his contemporaries to his extraordinary influence; and if it has happened that this has been cited mainly from his colleagues and friends, it is not because it was lacking in other quarters. One of the most decided, and at the same time one of the most distinguished, of his political opponents was Sir Henry Hardinge, afterwards Governor-General of India. Sir Henry, who had on the first reading of the Reform Bill declared that public indignation must drive ministers from office immediately, declared after the Bill was passed, "It was Althorp carried the Bill. His fine temper did it. Once, in answer to a most able and argumentative speech of Croker, he rose and merely observed that 'he had made some calculations which he considered as entirely conclusive in refutation of the right honourable gentleman's arguments, but unfortunately he had mislaid them, so that he could only say that if the House would be guided by his advice they would reject the amendment'—which they did accordingly. There was no standing against such influence as this."

Charles Greville, more prone to disparagement than to praise of the public men of his time, in reviewing Althorp's career just after his death, has written of him thus: "He exercised in the House of Commons an influence, and even a dominion, greater than any leader either after or before him. Neither Pitt the father nor Pitt the son, in the plenitude of their magnificent dictatorships, nor Canning in the days of his most brilliant displays of oratory and wit, nor Castlereagh, returning in all the glory of an ovation from the overthrow of Napoleon, could govern with the same sway the most unruly and fastidious assembly that the world ever saw. His friends followed this plain and simple man with enthusiastic devotion, and he possessed the faculty of disarming his political antagonists of all bitterness and animosity towards him; he was regarded in the House of Commons with sentiments akin to those of personal affection, with a boundless confidence and a universal esteem. Such was the irresistible ascendency of truth, sincerity, and honour, of a probity free from every taint of interest, of mere character unaided by the arts which captivate or subjugate mankind. This is the great practical panegyric which will consecrate the memory of Lord Althorp, and transmit it nobly to the latest posterity; but it is a panegyric not more honourable to the subject of it than to the national character which is susceptible of such impressions and acknowledges such influences. We may feel an honest pride and a happy confidence in the reflection that it is by such sterling qualities, by the simple and unostentatious practice of public and private virtue, that men may best recommend themselves to the reverence, the gratitude, and the affection of their countrymen, and be remembered hereafter as the benefactors of mankind."

It is, indeed, in a sense, the very absence of

brilliant and extraordinary characteristics in Althorp's mind that gives an especial interest to the study of his career. For it thereby appears that he played his leading and indispensable part in a great historic drama by virtue of instincts and qualities in which he was simply typical of the best and soundest instincts and qualities inherent among his fellow-countrymen. It is no less interesting, and much more surprising, to note that his complete neglect of all the arts, respectable or otherwise, of self-advancement habitually practised by politicians did not, as commonly happens, prevent his attainment of the place in which his country needed him. Each several arch of our constitutional history, bearing like an aqueduct the stream of national life, as it spans successive intervals of change, is composed of many stones of individual achievement, which gradually become lost to sight as they recede into the dark backward of time. But if, in the arch that typifies our peaceful Revolution of 1832, there are certain names deserving to be inscribed on the key stone, they are surely the names of Grey, of Russell, and of Althorp; and Althorp's is not the least memorable of the three.

Yet doubtless it is to be allowed that there is a further question that must needs suggest itself whenever the events of that epoch are recalled; a question that ought not here to be ignored, though for a full answer this can hardly be the place. It is the question—Of what real value was this great change, the first and all-important step toward the establishment of democracy in this State? Might not Althorp, and those who shared his great influence, have done better to repair and purify, as Wellington desired to do, the aristocratic form of government handed down to them, and to refrain from a too venturous attempt to

> "Cast the kingdoms old
> Into another mould"?

To this contention there is a double answer. In the first place, some change in the direction of democracy might even then be reasonably called inevitable, without abuse of that word so much abused by careless or cowardly politicians. This was a consequence both of the original nature and of the acquired powers of the representative House of Parliament. The predominant monarchy of the sixteenth century and much more the predominant nobility of the eighteenth had both made the House of Commons the instrument of their predominance. Thus they maintained and fostered an organ whose power would excel their own, whenever it should be animated by an independent life. Then, when the growth of the large towns had made the local inequalities of representation too glaring to be plausibly defended, the consequent redistribution of the elective franchise involved so great an extension of it that the result must necessarily be a democracy—that is, according to Austin's definition, "a government in which the governing body is a comparatively large fraction of the entire nation." The aristocratic government had existed under democratic forms, but after the first Reform Act the forms began to become realities. Whether Althorp would have welcomed the later Reform Acts of 1867 and 1885, with their extensions of power to an enormously larger "fraction of the nation," it is impossible to feel certain. Not much, perhaps, can be inferred on this point from the fact that we find him repeatedly alleging, after the Act of 1832 was passed, that in his opinion it had still left too much power to the landed interest; or from his declared inclination toward the adoption of the ballot in Parliamentary elections.

The motives which impelled him and most of his colleagues to desire and work for this democratic change were, in fact, eminently and characteristically practical; and a cordial approval of their work need not imply any theoretic preference or idealization of democracy in the abstract. It is even compatible with such cordial approval to hold that the ideal form of government is neither democracy nor monarchy, but aristocracy. The two other forms have, indeed, of late seemed to excite the most rhetorical and literary enthusiasm. The late Sir Henry Maine, in his deeply interesting book on "Popular Government," expresses his surprise at the frequent enthusiasm for democracy, regarding it as based, or mainly based, on the illusive expectation that democracies will be most active in legislative change. Here he somewhat ignores, it would seem, the naturally inspiring effect of the promise of equality, which democracy appears especially to hold out. Equality in many of its forms is a form also of justice, and justice is the highest aim of all political and social theory. But Plato found justice not in a democratic, but in a highly aristocratic Republic; and it is plain that the knowledge and political wisdom needed for good government can only reside in a small part of a community which recognizes as members of it the immense majority absorbed in providing for their material wants. Again, the idea of a short cut to national happiness by means of a good and wise despot has its natural attractions and plausibilities as an ideal form of government. But it is obviously far more difficult to secure the repeated transmission of the despot's goodness and wisdom to his successors than it need be to maintain the traditions of an aristocracy, as generation after generation is gradually renewed and trained. Plato, Milton, Auguste Comte, and almost all political idealists, have moulded their ideal commonwealths on an aristocratic type. A perfect aristocracy, with the rulers rightly carrying out their trust, should be the happiest and most really progressive as well as the most stable and powerful of States.

The justification of the English Reformers was that the English aristocratic government had, like all other aristocracies known to history, fallen very far short of any such perfection. It had, indeed, one superlative claim to put forward in its defence—the claim that under it the nation had issued triumphant from the long and terrible struggle against Napoleon. It may be doubted, however, whether this was due so much to the tenacity of an aristocracy as to the tenacity of the English race, and to its production of such men as Nelson and Wellington to save their masters from the consequences of the blundering and indecision into which those masters repeatedly relapsed. A democratic England would very possibly have discovered her great captains at least as soon, and supported them more warmly when discovered. So in the preceding generation it was the elder Pitt, a man of the middle classes by descent, and with the middle classes supporting him, who swept aside the party conflicts of a degenerate oligarchy, and crowned his country with the revived glories of the times of Cromwell and Marlborough. But even if the absorption in the great war against Napoleon be accepted as excuse for the neglect of many internal reforms involving systematic change, it cannot excuse neglect of essential safeguards of the system as it stood. The strenuous and disciplined spirit, which alone can maintain a strong aristocracy, was in too great measure lacking. This was apparent as much in social habits as in political administration. Althorp had had abundant proof of it even in circumstances touched on within the limits of this short book. In his earliest years, his father, though a man much above the average in intelligence and accomplishment, left his son and heir to the company and training of servants. This may partly be accounted for by personal eccentricity, though even with such allowance it is not without further significance. But stronger proofs follow. What organs of national life, it may well be asked, can be of more vital interest to an aristocracy than the universities and the army, even if regarded only as training-grounds for the inheritors of power? Yet when Althorp goes to the university he finds regulations invented expressly, as it would seem, for the discouragement of men of rank from the discipline and interest of liberal studies. When he has entered Parliament, the first thing that moves him to decisive political action is the apathetic connivance of the Government and the ruling classes at a gross scandal in the highest places of the administration of the army. It was by such signs as these that Althorp and the Reformers of his time could read plainly that the old system had been weighed in its own balances and been found wanting.

Besides the vigilant preservation of its own strength and efficiency, an ideal aristocracy would of course provide diligently for the well-being of the classes excluded from political power. This is a function as likely, or more likely, to be neglected than the other; and that it had been neglected in these islands seemed to the Reformers of the time indisputable. It is often hard to separate natural from artificial causes of material misery. But that no slight part of the misery and degradation of the English poor could be removed by better laws and better administration, was proved by the Poor Law and Factory Acts of the Reformed Parliament. The evils of the old Poor Law were in themselves a condemnation of the Tory rule. Of all classes the rural poor should naturally have been the care of a government of landowners, and yet it was this very class that had to wait for the fall of that goverment to be rescued at the eleventh hour from ruin.

Political questions are habitually questions of choice between two alternatives, of which neither is without defect; and political sagacity consists in striking the balance of less and more. Perhaps at each of our three great democratic extensions of the franchise it may be fairly held that the arguments in favour of the change outweighed those against it; but it will be agreed by most that this may be more decidedly maintained of the Parliamentary Reform of 1832 than of either of the others that came after it. Its result was to give the chief influence in the State to the middle class; and whatever objections may be made to this disposal of power, it has at least the virtue which gained it the approbation of Aristotle, the virtue of superior stability, as well as of a just appreciation of the means to material prosperity. The moderate Conservative Peel became its most appropriate agent, and the commercial success of the middle of the nineteenth century its appropriate accompaniment. Yet this order too has had points in which it failed, and at any rate seems likely to yield place to another before it has had full opportunity of showing great qualities. It came well, on the whole, through some grave trials, such as the Indian Mutiny and the famines in Ireland and Lancashire; but severer tests are probably in store for the untried State which is being developed from it.

The second part of the twofold answer to those who deprecate the initiative democratic change of 1832 must needs be of a less positive kind, and commending itself very differently to different minds. It is the answer based on an estimate of the social, economic, and moral elements of the British State; elements which, though by no means wholly impervious to change, are at least more intrinsically and naturally enduring than forms of government. If in these elements are to be found qualities such as promise security against the recognized dangers of democracy, they may go far to justify those who began and those who have continued or are continuing the change.

Invasion of the rights of property on the one hand, and, on the other, intellectual stagnation at a dead level under the despotism of a majority, appear to be the dangers of democratic institutions that are now most commonly dwelt upon. As to the former, we may, it would seem, derive some reassurance from the example not only of the United States but also of France, where universal suffrage has fortified the rights of landed proprietors (these being, of course, in great part peasants), and moreover has abstained even from levying an income tax on the substance of the well-to-do minority. And while it is characteristic of the English people that compassion has long made their Poor Laws more socialistic than elsewhere, it is no less characteristic of that people to abhor any extended form of socialism which will seriously affect industrial enterprise. Enjoyment of the rights of individual ownership is fully as keen in our industrial classes as in any others, and also the imperative demand for free opportunity of individual advancement. "That Christian men's goods are not common" will probably be as enduring an Article of Religion in England as any of the other thirty-eight. There may be more legislation of a socialist tinge to come, but there hardly seems yet to be reasonable ground for doubting that, logically or illogically, it will stop short of anything gravely injurious to national industry. If not, then the race will have changed the nature which has been increasingly inherent in it for at least three centuries; and this is a change not easily or swiftly made.

In many respects a better forecast of the future of our own democracy may perhaps be formed from the example of the kindred people of the United States than from any other; but here too there are many differences, of both favourable and unfavourable comparison. On the one hand, the as yet enormous space and physical resources of the United States simplify political problems and mitigate political evils. On the other hand, the very lack of these resources in the old country may have its good side. It makes classes of the community more interdependent, with more opportunity for mutual help, and brings home to all the better endowed in whom conscience is not dead the imperative truth, *Richesse oblige*. It is, in fact, on the recognition of that truth by the upper classes of these islands that their fate and the fate of their country in great part depends. There is still here a far more general recognition than in America of the importance to the community of a class possessing leisure ; a possession which, however it may be wasted or abused by some, is essential to the independent intellectual progress of a State. The desire of money flourishes in all human communities, and must flourish. The thing to be hoped and striven for is that at least other desires should be maintained to the utmost in competition ; not only the desire of virtue, which is good in itself, but the desires of knowledge, fame, influence, leisure, art, social refinement, variety of intercourse and experience. The plea urged in extenuation of the mercenary corruption of politics in the United States, is that men cannot be expected to work for nothing, and that money there is the equivalent of social prominence here, the politician's desire being equally self-regarding in either case. There is truth in this ; yet (in default of devotion such as Althorp's) the motive of ambition must surely be preferred to that of avarice. The practical answer to the plea is the admitted fact that, although there exists in the United States, as in this country and in all civilized communities, a true aristocracy of education, manners, and character, yet this class is found to hold aloof almost entirely from politics there, while here such abstention occurs in a far smaller degree. This advantage is doubtless found to be quite compatible here with the influence of discreditable politicians, but in itself it is valuable, and we could ill afford its diminution.

Cromwell wrote to a friend in the midst of the great civil war, "I had rather have a plain russet-coated captain that knows what he fights for, and loves what he knows, than that which you call a gentleman, and is nothing else. I honour a gentleman that is so indeed." The idea is not very logically expressed, but the meaning is plain, and it is the expression of a feeling that exists, and, it is to be hoped, will always exist, in the English people—the cheerful and unenvious recognition of differences of station between man and man, but a recognition expecting such differences to be justified by personal qualities. In this country the most highly styled of the nobility would be ashamed to deny that to be a gentleman is more than to be a nobleman, and that it is as possible to be the second of these things and not the first, as it is to be the first and not the second.

It is this honourable impulse to respect the results of discipline in character, manners, and understanding that should prove, if not swamped or betrayed, one of the most valuable securities in this country against the venality and vulgarity that have sometimes soiled the reputation of democracy.

Some of the fears caused by democratic change have, so far at least, proved to be somewhat exaggerated. The democracies arising immediately from violent revolution in France and in Spanish America were, indeed, darkly coloured by their origin and circumstances. But beyond these it can hardly be said that democracies have shown themselves fierce and bloodthirsty, or even intolerant of free thought or of the rights of minorities in general. History has few more splendid examples of national clemency than that of the United States toward the defeated seceders of the South. The most formidable dangers of democracy seem more likely to be due to the defects, so to speak, of its head than to those of its heart. Its tendency in many instances is rather to be too tolerant of enemies and evils of the State, or at least to be disastrously or dangerously late in taking precautions against them. By importunities and cajoleries it may be led unperceiving past the point where concession should have been decisively denied. The long-suffering of the United States toward the continued encroachments of the slave-holding interest before the Secession is an example of this tendency, and of its catastrophic results. Even since their great war the Americans have relapsed into a dangerous toleration, not of the mere existence, but of the actual dominance of vote-trucking, anti-national organizations. Democratic constituencies have neither the knowledge to realize nor the leisure to attend closely to increasing political dangers, and may wait till these are huge enough to involve some national convulsion, in which the heedless giant at last puts forth his strength. Till then agitations menacing the State are apt to be tolerated, or even rather enjoyed by the masses looking on, as supplying a diversion from the dulness of ordinary life. "C'est avec le lendemain que mon esprit lutte," was a saying of Metternich's; and to statesmen who have better and more hopeful causes than Metternich's to maintain, that struggle is not less but even more requisite. It is here that they will have to defend democracy against its own negligence. The great danger to be dreaded now for our democratic State, would seem to be neither the military tyranny foreboded by Huskisson and other opponents of Reform in 1830—a fear which hitherto has seemed almost an absurdity—nor yet from the overbearing of the majority; but rather from the conspiracies of active and organized minorities, predominant in some locality or class, and preying by sufferance on the inert commonwealth. It is partly to guard against these that it is of imperative need to retain the political service of classes possessing more knowledge and a wider outlook than are possible to the great bulk of the nation. But it is hardly less necessary toward this end that artificial privileges should give way, as they have been giving way ever since the Reform Act of 1832. It is only thus that the great end can now be secured of the recognition of the indivisible unity of the State. The one essential thing is that the commonwealth should be indeed a commonwealth, that is, a State in which all forces are both encouraged and constrained to work together for the good of the whole, not for this or that section to the damage or danger of the rest. It is plain to-day that what most needs defence is the true republican principle in the highest sense of that word—the principle that if a people is to be free and great, if its laws are to be a means toward true national life, no local or sectional animosities or covetousnesses, whether of landlords or of tenants, of manufacturers or of agriculturists, of Protestants or of Roman Catholics, of Churchmen or of Dissenters, of employers or of employed, of rich or of poor, are to escape and prevail against the just control of the general sense and purpose of the commonwealth.

It is to the realization and consolidation of a republic in this sense that our country will for some time chiefly have to muster all her available forces against the selfish and disintegrating elements at work. All political science and art, all statesmanship in any high sense, must rest on the understanding that one part of the community cannot be veritably benefited or injured without benefit or injury to the rest. If this be not so, then a State becomes little better than a concourse of savage tribes perpetually at war beneath a semblance of civilization and peace. It is the classes with leisure and education who are chiefly bound to comprehend and realize this, and to contribute that political wisdom which needs knowledge as well as common sense, wide sympathy as well as equitable intention. The prospect of their making this contribution in due measure will depend very greatly, though not altogether, on themselves. Their use will be lost to the common weal if they lapse generally into the luxury, frivolity, and vulgar self-conceit in which a part of them—a small part perhaps, but not the least conspicuous—are at once ludicrously and lamentably immersed; or again, if the democracy permits itself to fall into the hands of selfish or fanatical intriguers, substituting the bribery of classes for that of individuals, and using the very machinery whereby knowledge might be spread to distort fact and darken counsel. But on both these points there is much ground for hope of the better event, though as yet it is a hope needing confirmation. Nor should it be forgotten that the increasing complexity of modern civilization demands continually a correspondingly increasing body of trained and skilled administrators, such as of itself furnishes a corrective element of aristocracy, though of too "bureaucratic" a kind to be wholesomely trusted as a sole or principal security.

Besides these vaguer safeguards inherent in the social structure of the community, in the "ancient and inbred" qualities of the race, it will also probably be needful to discover some more defined and statutory means of augmenting the stability of the Constitution, which is now liable to fundamental change at the bidding of a simple majority of one legislative Chamber. To expect the efficient discharge of this conservative function from the present second Chamber would plainly be a ruinous delusion. While the House of Lords, as at present constituted, is a standing provocation to revolutionary impulses, it is an illusive and futile barrier against them. It can prevent or obstruct the less conspicuous, though often highly important, legislative measures, but it is powerless to withstand the greater changes which are sometimes all the more likely to be demanded in consequence of the repeated frustration of the less. This was so, as we have seen, even in 1832.

It would doubtless have been expedient at that epoch to have introduced into our polity some of the constitutional safeguards of the United States; of which safeguards the requirement of a two-thirds majority for a constitutional amendment appears to be perhaps the simplest and easiest to imitate. But any such imitation would probably have found little support from either Liberals or Tories, unaccustomed at that time to look to the American Republic for conservative securities. To the group of alienate Englishmen who drew up the Constitution of the United States, these securities were naturally suggested by the new and strange field in which they worked. But in the mother-country it would have needed a far more unusual degree both of foresight and of determination to introduce, much more to establish, such safeguards at the time of the first Reform Act. Now, however, the discussion of them is becoming comparatively familiar, and it may be hoped that in no long time they may be introduced on the safer foundation of a general sense of their necessity. Another aid of stability, as well as of justice, would be found in a system of proportional representation, which is, in fact, a deduction from the principle of democracy in its best form. The adoption of such provisions as these would be a further vindication of the Reformers of sixty years ago, as tending to prove that the road they chose was that likely to lead to fewest and most defeasible dangers, and as justifying their bold trust in the sobriety and sagacity of their fellow-countrymen.

But constitutional and organic change of any kind, even with the object of constitutional security, and for self-protection of a democracy, is a difficult and delicate task; and the wisdom and character of the men who take the lead at such times must always be of incalculable importance. Happily, there have not been many times in the history of England when her home affairs have been in so disordered or critical a state as to need the commanding genius of an individual man to set them straight. Since Cromwell's time there has been perhaps only one English statesman, the elder Pitt, to whom commanding genius, of a political kind, can properly be attributed ; and in him it showed itself chiefly in the foreign policy that added so many mansions to the stately house of British Empire. But the task of a British statesman at home is not to create, but to preserve and to develope. It is not so much brilliance or originality that is needed in him as instinctive sympathy with the genius of his people and their best traditions, intellectual fairness and clear sight, sincerity of purpose, steadiness, but not obstinacy, of will. Both great parties of the State have in this generation shown that they may mistake an ingenious rhetorician for a great statesman ; and one at least of those parties has grievously answered that grievous fault. When England is tired of being governed by histrionic orators she may finally decide—perhaps is already gradually deciding—to recur to rulers of a more serviceable sort.

We do not require a Bismarck, or even a Cavour, still less any spurious counterfeit of such; but men with certain of the best qualities of these statesmen in forms more indigenous to British soil; men resolute but patient and self-controlled, "rich in saving common sense," firm in wielding power, but with no covetousness of power for itself. Such men have led us before, and may yet lead us again. This, at least, may be said here in conclusion, that in whatever crisis may yet be reserved by destiny for our country, it will indeed be well for her if she can be served once more at her need by such men as he whose loyal service these pages are written to recall; the "most frank, true, and stout-hearted of God's creatures," the Englishman whose wisdom and courage helped England through the perils of a mighty change, the leader whom his friends and followers knew among themselves by the honoured and cherished name of "honest Jack Althorp."

If he could hear men praise him for the unique disinterestedness of his public life, he would doubtless deny himself all credit for it, on the ground that he had no temptation to the artifices of political ambition, because his heart was primarily not in these matters, but rather in the simple interests of his country home. Truly it was so, but to know the cause nowise impairs our prizing the effect; and if he is thus to escape admiration of his freedom from self-seeking, it must all the more fall to him for the large devotion of his uncongenial and harassing labour for the State. He came out of the fields and woods, and to the fields and woods he returned; but while he remained in the hot and dusty atmosphere of political strife, it was freshened by the homely chivalry of his nature, as a crowded hall might be freshened by some far-borne breath of the pure free air he loved. Men of all parties felt the better for his presence among them then; men of all parties may feel the better for his memory among us now.

THE END.

PRINTED BY WILLIAM CLOWES AND SONS, LIMITED,
LONDON AND BECCLES. *J. D. & Co.*

www.ingramcontent.com/pod-product-compliance
Lightning Source LLC
Chambersburg PA
CBHW020803230426
43666CB00007B/836